Empowering English Language Learners

THE HOUSE OF PRISCA AND AQUILA

Our mission at the House of Prisca and Aquila is to produce quality books that expound accurately the word of God to empower women and men to minister together in a multicultural church. Our writers have a positive view of the Bible as God's revelation that affects both thoughts and words, so it is plenary, historically accurate, and consistent in itself, fully reliable, and authoritative as God's revelation. Because God is true, God's revelation is true, inclusive to men and women and speaking to a multicultural church, wherein all the diversity of the church is represented within the parameters of egalitarianism and inerrancy.

The word of God is what we are expounding, thereby empowering women and men to minister together in all levels of the church and home. The reason we say women and men together is because that is the model of Prisca and Aquila, ministering together to another member of the church at Apollos: Having heard Apollos, Priscilla and Aquila took him aside and more accurately expounded to him the Way of God. (Acts 18:26). True exposition, like true religion, is by no means boring it is fascinating. Books that reveal and expound God's true nature burn within us as they elucidate the Scripture and apply it to our lives.

This was the experience of the disciples who heard Jesus on the road to Emmaus: Were not our hearts burning while Jesus was talking to us on the road, while he was opening the scriptures to us? (Luke 24:32). We are hoping to create the classics of tomorrow, significant and accessible trade and academic books that burn within us.

Our house is like the home to which Prisca and Aquila no doubt brought Apollos as they took him aside. It is like the home in Emmaus where Jesus stopped to break bread and reveal his presence. It is like the house built on the rock of obedience to Jesus (Matt 7:24). Our house, is as a euphemism for our publishing team, is a home where truth is shared and Jesus Spirit breaks bread with us, nourishing all of us with his bounty of truth.

We are delighted to work together with Wipf and Stock in this series and welcome submissions on a wide variety of topics from an egalitarian, inerrantist global perspective.

For more information, see our Web site:
https://sites.google.com/site/houseofpriscaandaquila/.

Empowering English Language Learners

Successful Strategies of Christian Educators

EDITED BY

JEANNE C. DeFAZIO

WILLIAM DAVID SPENCER

WIPF & STOCK · Eugene, Oregon

EMPOWERING ENGLISH LANGUAGE LEARNERS
Successful Strategies of Christian Educators

Wipf & Stock
An Imprint of Wipf and Stock Publishers
199 W. 8th Ave., Suite 3
Eugene, OR 97401

www.wipfandstock.com

PAPERBACK ISBN: 978-1-5326-4001-8
HARDCOVER ISBN: 978-1-5326-4002-5
EBOOK ISBN: 978-1-5326-4003-2

Manufactured in the U.S.A.

BY THE SAME AUTHORS

DEAN BORGMAN

A History of American Youth Ministry (Benson and Senter's The Complete Book of Youth Ministries)

Encyclopedia of Youth Studies (www.centerforyouth.org)

Bridging the Gap: From Social Science to Congregations, Researchers to Practitioners

Eugene Roehlkepartain et al.'s "The Handbook of Spiritual Development in Childhood and Adolescence"

When Kumbaya Is Not Enough: A Practical Theology for Youth Ministry

Hear My Story: Understanding the Cries of Troubled Youth

Foundations for Youth Ministry: Theological Engagement with Teen Life and Culture

JENNIFER MARIE CREAMER

God as Creator in Acts 17:24

JEANNE C. DEFAZIO

Creative Ways to Build Christian Community (ed. with John P. Lathrop)

How to Have an Attitude of Gratitude on the Night Shift (with Teresa Flowers)

Redeeming the Screens (ed. with William David Spencer)

Berkeley Street Theatre: How Improvisation and Street Theater Emerged as Christian Outreach to the Culture of the Time (editor)

SEONG HYUN PARK

Reaching for the New Jerusalem: A Biblical and Theological Framework for the City (ed. with W. D. Spencer and A.B. Spencer)

OLGA SOLER

Just Don't Marry One (contributing author)

Tough Inspirations from the Weeping Prophet (preface: Kevin Kirkpatrick)

Apocalypse of Youth (Artist Harriet Nesbitt as told to Olga Soler)

Creative Ways to Build Christian Community (contributing author)

Epistle to the Magadalenes (author and illustrator)

Redeeming the Screens (contributing author)

Berkeley Street Theatre: How Improvisation and Street Theater Emerged as Christian Outreach to the Culture of the Time (contributing author)

The First Book: Nature, The Second Book: Time Travel, Adventure, Romance, Faith, The Third Book: Revelation: Revelations Series

AÍDA BESANÇON SPENCER

Beyond the Curse: Women Called to Ministry (trans. into French and Spanish)

The Global God (ed. with W. D. Spencer)

Global Voices on Biblical Equality (ed. with W. D. Spencer and M. Haddad)

God through the Looking Glass (ed. with W. D. Spencer)

The Goddess Revival (with C. Kroeger, D. Hailson, and W. D. Spencer)

Joy Through the Night (with W. D. Spencer)

Latino Heritage Bible (ed. with others)

Marriage at the Crossroads (with W. D. Spencer, S. R. Tracy, and C. G. Tracy)

Paul's Literary Style: A Stylistic and Historical Comparison of II Corinthians 11:16-12:13, Romans 8:9-39, and Philippians 3:2-4:13

The Prayer Life of Jesus (with W. D. Spencer)

Reaching for the New Jerusalem (with S. H. Park and W. D. Spencer)

Second Corinthians. Bible Study Commentary (with W. D. Spencer) (trans. into Chinese)

Second Corinthians: Daily Bible Commentary

1 Timothy (New Covenant Commentary Series)

2 Timothy and Titus (New Covenant Commentary Series)

WILLIAM DAVID SPENCER

Name in the Papers (A Novel)

Mysterium and Mystery: The Clerical Crime Novel

Dread Jesus

Redeeming the Screens (ed. with J. C. DeFazio)

God through the Looking Glass: Glimpses from the Arts (ed. with A.B. Spencer)

Marriage at the Crossroads: Couples in Conversation about Discipleship, Gender Roles, Decision Making and Intimacy (with A.B. Spencer, S.R. Tracy and C.G. Tracy)

Joy through the Night: Biblical Resources on Suffering (with A.B. Spencer)

The Prayer Life of Jesus: Shout of Agony, Revelation of Love (with A.B. Spencer)

Global Voices on Biblical Equality: Women and Men Serving Together in the Church (ed. with A.B. Spencer and M. Haddad)

Reaching for the New Jerusalem: A Biblical and Theological Framework for the City (ed. with S.H. Park and A.B. Spencer)

The Global God: Multicultural Evangelical Views of God (ed. with A.B. Spencer)

The Goddess Revival: A Christian Response (with A.B. Spencer, D.G.F. Hailson and C. Kroeger)

Chanting Down Babylon: The Rastafari Reader (ed. with N.S. Murrell and A.A. McFarlane)

2 Corinthians: A Commentary (with A.B. Spencer)

GEMMA WENGER

Creative Ways to Build Christian Community (contributing author)

Redeeming the Screens (contributing author)

This book is dedicated to all teachers and especially to those who made a difference in my life: Dr. William David Spencer at The Center For Urban Ministerial Education, Gordon Conwell Theological Seminary, Dr. Aída Besançon Spencer at Gordon Conwell Theological Seminary, Dr. Stylianos Spryidakis at the University of California, Davis Campus, Sister M. Aquinas Nimitz O.P. at Dominican University of San Rafael, Dr. Ali Asani at Harvard University School of Religion, Dr. Marie Johnstone of CalState Teach Program at California State University of Fullerton, Dr. Jane Kappel, Cal State Teach Program at California State University of Fresno, Mr. Blodgett at Davis High School, Davis California. Among my peers, I benefited from the teaching advice of my brother, Peter DeFazio, who for the past 30 years has taught English to Japanese students in Japan and in the United States. As an experienced teacher of English Language Learners from culturally diverse backgrounds in the primary grades, my beloved and belated cousin, Lynn Jacobs Massetti shared key strategies which I practiced to successfully complete my California Teaching Credential Program. Likewise, my niece, Francesca Reinhard, a talented teacher, graciously shared from her teaching experiences techniques which encouraged me greatly while I completed my Teaching Program in 2008. Adrienne DeFazio, my sister in law, explained with great humor and insight her strategies to enhance English learning in the inner city classroom. A great mentor as a teacher is my cousin, Susan Kasimatis, who shared ways to classroom manage and keep middle school English Language Learners engaged. Chris Hodgkins has been a great inspiration to me as a scholar and author. I am grateful to all of you.

Jeanne DeFazio

Contents

Acknowledgements

Jeanne DeFazio

A LOT OF HARD work went into making this book. It was inspired by the creative genius of Drs. William David and Aída Besançon Spencer of the House of Prisca and Aquila Series that is published by Wipf and Stock. Thank you to Dr. William David Spencer for reading the manuscript and making helpful suggestions. The text was brilliantly polished and perfected by its editor: Mary Riso. Matthew W. Martens editorial skills helped tremendously. Cherry Gorton served as a trusted consultant to this work. This book exists because of those who added their stories to mine: Dean Borgman, Jennifer Creamer, Julia Davis, Jan and Michael Dempsey, Jean Dimock, Olga Soler, Seong Hyun Park, Aída Besançon Spencer, William David Spencer, Virginia Ward and Gemma Wenger.

I would like to give a shout of praise to all of the following for constantly reminding me I can do better: my niece Ella Louise Ryan, a talented and beautiful young actress, Beth Behrs and SheHerd Power for bringing healing to the hurting, Susan Stafford, founder of Wheel of Grace Unlimited as she cares for those who are sick and dying, Ted Baehr and his awesome ministry via MovieGuide®, stuntman Bob Yerkes whose reward in heaven will be great for his generosity of spirit, hospitality and humor, Larry Abernathy and Linda Bair Smith who share the love of Jesus each week on the Cathedral of Love Live Stream broadcast, Bob Rieth and his wonderful wife Marion, whose Media Fellowship International shines the light in the entertainment industry. Joanne Petronella with her ministry team *Christ in You the Hope of Glory* who faithfully brings the Passion Play to the Via Dolorosa on Good Friday. First Lady Melania

Trump is a wonderful role model for English Language Learners. I am grateful to Peter Lynch at The Lynch Foundation who inspired me to take this project on. Special thanks to Caleb Loring III for his support of this book. I would like to thank Jesus most of all for his teaching that made this work possible.

Introduction

JENNIFER MARIE CREAMER

WHO IS MY NEIGHBOR? As it turns out, the neighbor in Jesus's parable of the Good Samaritan is the neighbor who is culturally different.[1] The Samaritans lived across the northern border of Judea. They were an ethnically diverse population from generations of assimilating those from other nations. The syncretistic religious practices of the Samaritans curried no favor with their neighbors to the south of their border. The Samaritan of the first century A.D. was looked upon with disdain by the Jews of Judea. Although the Jews of the first century viewed their Samaritan neighbors with distrust (and, perhaps, disdain), it was a Samaritan whom Jesus selected to be the hero of his story. It was the Samaritan and not the Jew of Jesus' immediate audience who demonstrated love to his neighbor. The Samaritan gave practical help to a person in need, at his own personal cost.

Who is our neighbor in today's world? It is the person born in El Salvador, in Morocco, in Bangladesh, in Cambodia, in the Caribbean or Pacific islands or in war zones who now find themselves in a foreign land. Our neighbor may have left everything behind for a new start in a new country with a different language, different values, and a different culture. Nearly one out of every seven persons currently residing in the United States was born in another country.[2] Our neighbor has come to our doorstep. Even though there is much to be learned through cultural exchange, immigrants

---

1. Luke 10:25-37.

2. According to the Pew Research Center, 13.4% of the population of the United States was born in a foreign country. http://www.pewhispanic.org/2017/05/03/facts-on-u-s-immigrants-current-data/. Accessed 22 November 2017.

are, all too often, either ignored or treated with disrespect by society at large. How can we better follow Jesus' mandate to love our neighbors?

Empowering English Language Learners explicates one way that we can love our neighbors: through providing quality education to those seeking to learn English, or to learn other subjects through the medium of the English language. Immigrants from non-English speaking nations need to learn English to succeed in school, to find a job, and to become naturalized citizens. No matter how advanced the level of education in the home country, an immigrant will need to learn English to find decent employment. Even a doctor or an engineer with advanced degrees in his or her home country may be offered only menial jobs in the United States until sufficient English has been mastered. Children need English to succeed in school and to make new friends. Those adults and children crossing language and cultural boundaries in our classes need masterful teachers to encourage and instruct them.

Empowering English Language Learners is not just another book on teaching theory. Teaching theory is important, indeed, and it is discussed. What is different about this volume is that it discusses teaching strategy as evaluated through personal experience. Each contributor is a veteran educator. This book overflows with the wealth of over two hundred years of cumulative teaching experience. Each chapter refracts teaching strategy through the lens of practical experience. With candor and insight gleaned from their years spent in the classroom, the authors explain what works. And, sometimes, they also explain what does not work. This book reflects the enormous diversity in student populations and teaching assignments. The chapters in this book cover an array of educational settings, from preschool to graduate school, and from secular public schools to private Christian schools, as well as in-house church programs.

Contributing authors who identify strategies of Christian teachers in a secular setting include Olga Soler, Gemma Wenger, and Julia Davis. Olga Soler writes her chapter, "Bridge Builders" with the unique perspective of being a second-generation immigrant, herself. She highlights the immigrant experience and the need for empathy, creativity, and use of an interactive teaching style to build a bridge to those who may experience fear of the dominant culture as well as loss of their home culture. In "Modeling Success in the Inner-City Classroom from a Christian Perspective," Gemma Wenger details her personal evaluation of the effectiveness of various methods facilitated in public, kindergarten-12th grade settings from her perspective as a teaching specialist for many years in difficult, lower so-cio-economic schools. She makes a compelling argument in favor of using different teaching techniques for both English language learners and learn-ers of standard English. In "Strategies That Are Scripturally Based for the Public School Classroom," Julia Davis integrates Scripture as a framework for the teaching practices she employs as a thirty-year veteran teacher in inner-city schools. She discusses classroom management, the importance of first impressions, the need for teachers to practice self-care, teachers as role models, and the place of structure and rules in the classroom.

Jean Dimock, in her chapter, "Instructing English Language Learners in a Secular College," lays as a foundation the principle of showing hos-pitality to strangers. She describes her approach as one of showing care for the student: expressing appreciation for those who take courses in English when English is not their mother-tongue, understanding the stu-dent's home culture, teaching study skills, and providing appropriate help and referrals for those who struggle in class. Michael and Jan Dempsey, in their chapter "ESL-Volunteer Programs in Churches and Public Libraries," make a strong case that teaching English to recent immigrants is a form of Christian hospitality. They chronicle their experience of teaching English to refugees in volunteer settings, including programs at libraries, as well as the burgeoning language program with multiple levels of instruction that they facilitate at their local church with volunteer teachers.

Contributing authors who identify strategies of Christian teachers in a Christian setting include Jeanne DeFazio, Dean Borgman, Virginia Ward, William Spencer and Seong Park. Jeanne DeFazio's chapter, "Teach-ing Migrant Children Prepared Me to Teach Theology to At-Risk English Language Learners" is informed by her nine years of experience of assisting students in seminary theology courses as well as her academic background in education. She stresses the importance of prayer, repetition of content, and creating a "happy mistake zone" to intentionally reduce student anxiety. In "Dialogical Teaching in the Digital Age," Dean Borgman writes about relational teaching and the need for a holistic approach based on love. His reflections include the impact of the screen on the emerging generation: to-day's students want to discover information through beneficial interactions. Virginia Ward discusses the seminary classroom as "learning labs for ELL students" in her chapter entitled "English Language Learners as Paceset-ters." She describes the various types of students who enroll in her seminary classes and gives practical suggestions for those teaching in multi-cultural seminary contexts, including the facilitation of group projects, the importance of clear communication, and learning about the various ethnicities represented in the class. William Spencer, likewise, details practical suggestions for the multi-cultural seminary classroom. In his chapter, "Intentional Teaching," he describes how he manages classrooms with students from varied educational backgrounds: he creates a multi-level teaching approach by providing support to at-risk students, showing value to normally-paced students, and seeking to encourage more advanced students while, at the same time (and in the same classroom), training teaching assistants as future faculty. Finally, in "Language of Seminary Classroom and the Language of the City," Seong Park details the needs of the growing immigrant population of Boston. With the influx of immigrants to the city, the number of churches has increased exponentially. Park discusses how the seminary may best serve the needs of immigrant churches.

Each author in this book brings to the table a unique background as well as rich insights, from which all instructors may learn. A common thread woven throughout the ten chapters is a sense of respect for the student and care for the individual.

It is a tragic misconception that a person is not intelligent if they struggle with English. In my own experience, I have consistently found the English language learners to be some of the brightest and most motivated students in my classes. They know that they need to study and work hard. They may, however, struggle with English grammar. One of the sharpest college level students I have encountered in nearly thirty years of teaching had only an eighth-grade education in a language other than English. Priyanka[3] had been pulled out of school by her family at an early age to do domestic work. Sure, she made plenty of spelling and grammar mistakes on her papers, she had taught herself English. Yet, her work was consistently more insightful than those students who came to my class already holding master's degrees. Another student, Rajiv, approached me after the first day of class with fear in his eyes and on the verge of tears. "Sister," he said, "I don't know if I can pass this course. English is my ninth language. And I taught myself." Sure enough, Rajiv failed to achieve a passing grade on his first few assignments due to lack of facility with the English language. After several weeks, however, his grades began to improve steadily. While his classmates took coffee breaks, Rajiv sat at his desk and worked. While his classmates played soccer, Rajiv sat at his desk and worked. While his

3. Names are changed.

classmates talked late and laughed long, Rajiv sat at his desk and worked. Rajiv considered carefully the comments that were made on his graded assignments. He made improvements week by week. When he didn't understand something, he would turn up at my door to ask for help. Through great determination, Rajiv completed the course with a grade above the class average. He is a testament to sheer hard work and discipline a lesson that many of my English-only students would do well to consider.

Those who teach or encounter English language learners in other settings will find much to ponder in the chapters that follow. Teachers and students of education will find *Empowering English Language Learners* to be particularly helpful, as will students, ministers, volunteers, and all who cross paths with people of different backgrounds. All who seek to love their multicultural neighbors will be enriched by this volume.

Part One:

Strategies of Christian Teachers
in a Secular Setting

Chapter One

Jeremiah 29:7
Bridge Builders

OLGA SOLER

MY EXPERIENCE AS A teacher has served both the immigrant and the dominant culture. I have taught English as a Second Language to pre-K through twelfth grade students in the inner city to minorities in Fitchburg, Massachusetts, taught Spanish in the suburbs of Keene, Texas and Holden, MA, and worked with those of affluence who had learning difficulties in Sudbury, MA. As a second-generation immigrant, I had a unique perspective in all my teaching situations informed not only by my education but by my own experience as student in the inner city. I also did a stint in professional theater in New York, ran my own licensed day care while my children were young, directed an itinerant ministry to the abused and addicted coast to coast, worked as a clinician in the human services and peppered it all with the performing and graphic arts. Teaching was the common thread through these diverse and multi-cultural experiences.

When you are second generation from another culture, you are born to be a special kind of teacher. You are born to be a bridge. This means you have one foot in the old world of your parents and the other in the new world to which you were born. The precipice you straddle is nothing to laugh at. You often long to leave one side and join the other, but bridges are so necessary. Being a bridge means being in a lonely place, but it also means you have a unique perspective. Like Moses, you are a stranger in a strange land, but you have a mission to build more bridges between the old and the new, the needy and resources, students and information and essentially from death to life.

As low-income kids from the South Bronx in New York City, my brother and I came up with an eleventh commandment; "Do what you can with what you got." So, I learned early to improvise, invent, and tell stories. These are primary teaching strategies as far as I am concerned, because teachers must learn to improvise to accommodate the diversity in their students and stories personalize knowledge, even those which may seem, at first, abstract to the student. The art of storytelling is an ancient one used to inspire. Data informs, but it seldom inspires, and, without inspiration, there is no motivation to learn.

Where the rudder of a human ship may be the mind, the inspiration is the wind in our sails. Inspiration moves us. Every good teacher knows motivation is everything. When we have so much content that there is no time for motivation, the outcome will not be favorable. The student will lose interest, not study regularly, and then cram. A UCLA study showed that spacing out learning was more effective than cramming for 90% of the participants.[1] Keeping students' interest throughout will inspire them to study regularly. If they cram, they may even be able to make succeed on a test, but what good will it do them in the long run if they do not retain their knowledge?

We are made to retain stories. Assistant professor of cinema arts in the Vanguard Sundance Program Aaron Daniel Annas put it this way, "Everything is based on story. If you are a math teacher and you are looking at one plus one equals two, your characters are One and One and your conflict is that they must add together. The solution of two resolves the story structure."[2] Even calculus, when viewed from the perspective of one's story, is far more engaging. This is why rabbis traditionally teach with stories and the Teacher of Teachers was the quintessential story teller.

When I had my day care on 81 acres of forest land in Sterling, MA, I brought the children outdoors every day, and I was constantly telling them stories that had to do with creation and nature. The experience of the children there was much like that of the children in the Forest schools of Denmark, which I will mention later. In his book *All I Really Need to*

1. Rosenthal, "Is Cramming for a Test Effective?," line 19.

2. Annas, "Story Telling as Teaching," podcast.

Know I Learned in Kindergarten,[3] Robert Fulghum told the truth. I learned the same lessons in my day care and my kids learned along with me. Some think Fulghum's book should be a guide for global leadership, and I agree with them because through sharing, storytelling, validation, respect for one another, valuing wonder and curiosity, and lots of finger paint, we learned. The children in my day care all grew up and in high school wrote compositions about our time together. My day care became part of their personal stories. They said it was the best time of their lives. Mine too. One even tattooed a favorite quotation from Shel Silverstein (one of our favorite authors at the day care) on her back. She is a good mother now and she is a close friend. The best learning is done in community. The best teachers are accessible, and the best students integrate what they have learned into their daily lives because they were taught well. The controversy of teaching values or not is a moot point. We teach them by modeling and storytelling whether we mean to or not. Therefore, we must strive to be good models and pick our stories well.

Being multilingual, I made myself useful to English speakers as a teacher of Spanish. Multilingual should go both ways and the best place to start is—preschool. When I was asked to teach a preschool Spanish class, I saw these little toddlers as the perfect students: "blank slates" or people who did not yet have any prejudices about who was better than who. They were happy to learn, and we got to it with happy songs, stories, and many role plays. And, by the way, we never grow out of multi-sensory education. When we learn on many sensory levels, it makes what we learn more permanent,[4] hence the value of a good power point presentation to adults.

Fifteen years later in the atrium of a large church, I met one of my students who had grown into a sophisticated lady. She hugged me tightly and informed me that my preschool Spanish class had saved her life. She was in a South American country acting as a liaison for an American company and an attack broke out that the military answered with helicopters, tanks, and guns. She was trapped in an office building with a non-English speaking woman, and they needed to communicate to get out. All she had was preschool Spanish but between that and sign language it was enough.

Most Americans are not multilingual. Some glibly tell others to learn English, but they do not learn other languages themselves. In Europe and Africa, it is not uncommon for people to speak 4 or 5 languages. If real

3. Fulghum, *All I Really Need to Know I Learned in Kindergarten.*
4. Quality Improvement Agency, "Teaching and Learning Programme."

education became a priority in this country, we would be multilingual. The point of a complete education is to have a knowledge of one's world that is well rounded. In a world of so many languages, being unilingual is very limiting. Bridges like we are have that gift to give to all people, a greater understanding through multiculturalism.[5] And even our students with learning disabilities ca33n benefit from this opportunity to expand their capability in unexpected ways since we are told that learning another language can help neurological connections in the brain.[6]

Another remarkable teaching assignment I had was a sixth grade class of mostly gifted young people. I attended this class as a substitute for a few days and told God to kill me before I ever had a class like this one again. Of course, the following year I had them as my home room class. They started off by demanding I answer why they needed to comply with what teachers said. I knew we would go nowhere till we covered this subject, and so we all sat on the floor and explored the ancient relationship between student and teacher. When we were done, they gave me a chair. I wanted to be respected, but the way I got respect was to model it by speaking to them as equals not underlings. Modeling is a fine method of teaching. People rebel when you say, "Do as I say and not as I do."

After that, we made that our style. They asked questions, and I asked questions in return, then we found the answers together as we examined our method of reasoning. I believe we call this the Socratic Method.[7] Eventually, we steered things towards the curriculum, and they all did splendidly and learned some critical thinking skills as well. A fringe benefit of this method was that in sharing the answers to our queries we became cohesive. I never countenanced exclusiveness or cliquishness, and we did have a few kids who didn't fit a mold easily. In the end, even these unusual ones felt included, and we became an enviable, supportive community. The young people began to help each other without my prompts. The creativity and cohesiveness were infectious. We had youth in other classrooms requesting to join our class.

If we are bilingual and multicultural, we will no doubt be employed at some point in a position that will use those skills. I wanted to teach drama,

---

5. Kruschewsky, "Multilingual Benefits That You Only Get If You Speak Another Language."

6. AThEME, "Morphological Awareness: Evidence for An Advantage of Bilingualism in Dyslexia (June 2017)."

7. The Foundation for Critical Thinking, "Socratic Teaching."

but administrators at inner city schools at which I applied felt the students had enough "drama" and they needed math and world history. I, therefore, became an ESL, Math, and World History teacher. My class consisted of 32 Hispanic and Hmong students ranging from 12 to 16 years of age. This assignment started in October because this group of children had scared away two other teachers already. The first thing these hostile adolescents told me was that they would get rid of me too. I lasted the rest of the year by the grace of God, but I lost so much weight I looked like a lamp stand. The stress was amazing.

With these kids there were times I got through and there were times I had to ask the ones who wanted to learn to sit up front and the rest to do what they wanted. I had to come to terms with the fact that I was not going to save all of them. I know why Karl Paul Reinhold Niebuhr might have formulated the prayer of serenity because his specialty, after all, was Christian Realism:

> *God, grant me the serenity*
> *To accept the things I cannot change,*
> *Courage to change the things I can,*
> *and wisdom to know the difference.*[8]

As teachers of this most precious but imperiled population of the poor in the inner city, we need to come to terms with our limitation. We will not build a Utopia on this earth, but we can make our corner of it better by leaving behind what positive impression that we can: a bit of wisdom, a good message for the soul, a show of respect or love in a time of need. We can't save everyone, but we can do something. When a lamb wanders into our pasture, we are responsible to give it a token at least that will sustain it to the next level. Who knows but what we leave may be just the thing to break a hole through the darkness.

With apologies to those who favor right or left, I am a moderate and also a shameless follower of Christ. I pray constantly for the creativity to improvise and innovate in a classroom whether it is in a suburban pre-school or the streets of the urban jungle. It is the best and only way I know of meeting the needs of so multifaceted and diverse an audience. I pray for the needs of each student. I pray their eyes be opened and their ears unstopped to all the good knowledge that surrounds them. I pray against the evil that would assail them. I also model learning. If I do not learn every

---

8. Brown, *The Essential Reinhold Niebuhr*, xv–xiv.

day from all those around me and from the One higher than I, then I have no right to require learning from others.

What we contend with in the inner city is formidable. It is difficult to teach those who need a therapist, and some well-adjusted friends, or food and shelter more than they need the three R's. Remember your educational psychology? Abraham Maslow saw that, when basic needs are not met and supports for survival are lacking, self-actualization and learning are practically impossible.[9] *Then Erik Erikson realized that trust must come before initiative, industry, and finally integrity or lasting dignity.*[10] *When we teach many of these children, we must remember to recognize survival priorities. We have to sustain life before we can enrich it.*

That is why Jesus fed the five thousand. He wanted them to learn and not faint. Children have difficulty learning when they don't have people who genuinely care for them, or when they don't have enough to eat, or when they are being abused. My experience in this rich country of ours is that teachers are underpaid, and, in addition, they end up buying many supplies they are not provided with to do their jobs. I found food therapy with a celebratory meal or treat was sometimes necessary to entice students to learn—even if we teachers had to foot the bill.

When you work in the inner city, you must get beyond the façade of toughness to the real heart of the student. You must develop some intense empathy. Empathy has to be a teaching strategy because you are dealing with a lot of trauma. Poverty, fear, immigration, cultural shock, abuse and PTSD, our fast-paced way of living, stultifying prejudice, learning difficulties, lack of books and funds for necessities and field trips, and much more stand between disadvantaged students and learning. They may feel very much like Tarzan coming out of the jungle. Don't blame them if they do not trust easily. Measure your words. Ask them lots of questions that show you care about them personally and not just delivering the material you need to teach.

When I started with my Fitchburg class, I found it to be disgracefully under-equipped. The class had no textbooks. The desks were carved with graffiti and the rug under our feet was moldy and torn. The message was clear: "You are not as important as the kids upstairs." And the class had received this message with venom. Their greeting to me was, "So you are from New York. Isn't that where they hang teachers out the window by their

9. Maslow, "A Theory of Human Motivation."

10. Cherry, "Erik Erikson's Stages of Psychosocial Development," *2795740.*

ankles?" I was enough of a New Yorker to recognize intimidation when I saw it, and to be honest I answered in kind. "Yeah, I was one of those kids who did that! Don't mess with me!" The answer like the question was mere posturing, but I learned this was not what was going to work with them. Adversaries only polarize.

"Mangos catch more flies than vinegar," and while people who have been demeaned and impoverished respect strength they also want to know that someone sees who they are. In order to teach them, I had to have many confrontations and many talks where I let them be heard as well as be talked at.

One young man, who oddly enough was named Angel, was a master of disruption. The mildest thing he did was put glue on all the seats before we came to class, which caused quite an uproar. He sabotaged the class at every turn—sometimes violently. He started the year with a solid "F," and we had to have a little talk one on one. He said his mother was a Christian and she said he was bound for hell.

I told him the last word on that had not been said and briefly explained the gospel, then I proceeded to give him some strategies for success —in my class at least. His behavior marginally improved, and he got a well-earned "A plus" in the next test. He was no fool.

During the next riot in class, the students were decrying the fact that they had to be in class at all because they were not learning anything. He was one of the loudest voices, of course, and I embarrassed him by asking, "So you are not learning anything, huh? Well, what grade did you get in the last test?" He hesitated. He would prove them all wrong (including himself) with the answer, but he was also too proud of that answer to keep it to himself, so, chagrined, he admitted to the *A plus* and the argument was over. We need compassion and the wisdom of God to teach the wounded sons and daughters of poverty. They have been scared, and they are angry, but there is genius there if we can coax it out.

Learn English sounds simple, doesn't it? We get this from people who did not bother to learn the language of the natives they displaced. It is true we need to learn the language of the dominant culture. But it's not so easy for all the above reasons and a few more. The immigrant's children know that this is not necessarily the ticket to paradise they are promised. They know this from others who have learned the language. This is not all the dominant culture wants from them. It wants them to assimilate; to forget who they are, including their names, their culture, and their way of life, and, when they do all this and try to become like them, it is still not good enough. They are still considered second-class citizens. This all seems like insanity to the immigrant, especially when the culture of the dominant race seems cold and hard to them. Why should they give up what they love for this?

It takes insight to sort through such questions and realize immigrants can learn a language but still be themselves. *Pedagogy of the Oppressed* [11] (Portuguese: *Pedagogia do Oprimido*), written by educator Paulo Freire, proposes a style of teaching with a new relationship between teacher, student, and society. My take away from Paulo's teaching was the use of the arts to help people see their own condition and think more critically about it. Having students collaborate to write a poem or a song, draw a picture, paint a mural, make a film, a play, a story about their condition helps them to put their problems out there where they can see them rationally with less emotional interference. It gives them pride of ownership and creatorship of the process as well. It is a great esteem builder, as well as a means of getting them to write and think and produce. Twelve years in school (if they make it that long) is not enough time to heal all their wounds. Helping them to look inside and question is more than many learn to do. It may be the way they will find their way out.

I have used this method with these kinds of students to great effect. I had three young men who were driving me crazy in class with their misbehavior. I discovered that they sang together for fun. I made a deal with them. If they behaved in my class, I would allow them to have a ten minute concert at the end of class. It was a win—win, and I'm still in touch with one of them who is now a technician at a recording studio in Washington State.

Many of these ghetto kids are abused; if not by family by their environment. Abuse breeds the need to control because the abused does not wish to return to the place where he or she is powerless. Control, however, produces rigidity and ruins relationships, and it is an armor that is hard to pierce. We can set firm limits in the classroom, but we must also give choices to students like this. That is allowing people to be who they are. It is not easy to do so, but it is possible. If we validate them for their feelings then redirect them so everyone can learn, we all get what we want. If we give people credit where credit is due, then show them how to succeed in the class, we will have more progress and less resistance.

---

11. Freire, *Pedagogy of the Oppressed.*

Dr. Ned Hallowell was a delight to work for. He is the Harvard expert on ADD/ADHD who has authored many books, including *Crazy Busy*[12] and *Super Parenting for ADD*[13] and *Driven to Distraction*.[14] As a medical man, he advocates for both medicine and alternatives in treating these conditions. I was his clinician for the alternative treatments of Dore and Learning Breakthrough neurological exercises, Reading Plus (exercise for the eyes), and Integrated Listening, a music-based program that works with gated and filtered classical music.

As a teacher, I was tired of trying to teach people who could not learn because of trauma or neurological impairments, and I was glad to be part of a healthy solution to at least one of these problems. I worked with children as well as adults. Important research has shown that movement and auditory stimulation are intimately connected to learning and, as I am a performing artist, this was good news to me.

The explosion of learning difficulties has captured the concern of the entire educational community. Pockets of problems like autism once appeared to be concentrated in areas like Princeton and Silicon Valley, but now, as diagnostic methods and information improve, we recognize them everywhere—in ghettos and prisons as well as in private and public schools. The success of people with these problems, of course, depends on their resources to cope with them.

12. Hallowell, *Crazy Busy.*

13. Hallowell, *Super Parenting for ADD.*

14. Hallowell, *Driven to Distraction.*

Learning difficulties like Dyslexia,[15] ADD/ADHD,[16] NVLD,[17] Autism[18] and others appear to be on the rise as are screen dependence and inactivity. There are many conjectures about this continuum of difficulties. Many feel these neurological problems are genetic, others epigenetic, and still others environmental, a mutation or heightened reaction to the pace of society. Different strains and types are being found and labeled, then the labels are removed, and they are generalized. Some even think these "disorders" are the next adaptive step for humankind, while others think that they are anachronistic, throwbacks to the primitive times when focusing attention on one object was fatal and only the multi-various survived the jungle's sudden death dangers. Spiritually speaking, they may be a reaction to the insane pace and chaos of our times. I think the answer may well be a little of all of the above. Medications are used to stimulate and then found to have side effects. Therapy helps because knowledge about our problems is always power, but it is not a complete cure. Alternative remedies are used like sensory therapy and occupational therapy. Movement and music is where I intersected with all this. I am a dancer, and I know the healing as well as entertainment and educational aspects of movement. At this point, even the experts don't have all the answers. Though the causes of the conditions have not yet been determined, much research is giving us some clues to what works to help these problems.

15. Dyslexia is a variable often familial learning disability involving difficulties in acquiring and processing language that is typically manifested by a lack of proficiency in reading, spelling, and writing. "Dyslexia," https://www.merriam-webster.com/dictionary/dyslexia.

16. Attention Deficit Disorder is a developmental disorder that is marked especially by persistent symptoms of inattention (such as distractibility, forgetfulness, or disorganization) or by symptoms of hyperactivity and impulsivity (such as fidgeting, speaking out of turn, or restlessness) or by symptoms of all three and that is not caused by any serious underlying physical or mental disorder. "Attention Deficit Disorder," https://www.merriam-webster.com/dictionary/attention%20deficit%20disorder.

17. "Many learning and attention issues create social challenges. But these are the main *symptoms of NVLD*. NVLD affects a child's social skills, but not his speech or writing skills. Children with NVLD tend to talk a lot, but they don't always share in a socially appropriate way. Or they might not relay the most important information. They often miss social cues, so making and keeping friends is a big challenge. There can also be misunderstandings with teachers, parents and other adults." Horowitz, "Nonverbal Learning Disabilities: A Primer."

18. Autism is a condition or disorder that begins in childhood and that causes problems in forming relationships and in communicating with other people. "Autism," http://learnersdictionary.com/definition/autism.

In Denmark, for example, the level of education across the board is very high. Attention disorders and disciplinary problems have been seen to respond well to Forest Schools, which is a method of using nature as the learning medium. These schools (much like my day care) favor a natural environment with all its exploration and climbing and music as major pedagogic strategies which provide much neurological development in balance, proprioception, and auditory stimulation.

Evidence that children being outdoors on a daily basis, all year round, benefits their learning and development has been documented in Scandinavia for over 20 years, and more recent studies in the UK corroborate the findings, which suggest that:

- Children's confidence is developed by them having the freedom, time, and space to learn and demonstrate independence.

- Social and emotional skills are increased by children gaining an awareness of the consequences of their actions on peers through team and paired activities that involve sharing, negotiating, and turn-taking.

- Children's communication and language development is increased through sensory experiences and using natural materials.

- Motivation and concentration is developed by children's fascination with nature; they are more attentive, have better powers of memory, and are less easily distracted.

- Physical skills are improved by children being outdoors, illustrated by evidence of better balance, agility, and strength.

- Children's health and immunity is strengthened through being outdoors regularly; they, along with teachers and other practitioners, seem to be ill less often.[19]

Similar experimental learning environments have been shown to mitigate learning difficulties in the UK and in the USA in a major study conducted with students with behavioral problems reported in "Environment as an Integrating Context for Learning" (EIC), where such programs caused fewer discipline problems with participants than experienced with their traditionally educated peers. [20]

19. Williams-Siegfredsen, "Danish Forest Schools," lines 96–108.

20. *Lieberman and Hoody,* "Closing the Achievement Gap. Using the Environment as an Integrating Context for Learning. Executive Summary."

Compare these healthier environments to those of our urban or even suburban schools. Is there any wonder we have as many learning problems as we do? Many of our children spend hours in front of screens instead of exploring the real world and even now are beginning to be taught by screens instead of teachers in on-line classes on the elementary and middle school levels. Such practices have been shown to have a real impact on the brain, especially the cerebellum which has to do with motor function.[21] The good news is movement can help it develop properly. Books like *Teaching with the Brain in Mind* by Eric Jensen outline many ways movement can help. Balance movement, figure eights, such as those we used in the Dore program, and aerobic movement in particular have good effects on the brain.

On the west coast, Ann Green Gilbert has revolutionized several school districts with her program called *Brain Dance*—a series of 8 types of movement that simulate the movement of normal infants through toddlerhood. These have been seen to assist in improved brain activity as well as balance and stability for senior citizens as well as people of all ages. I found her to be very generous with her knowledge, and she makes her simple exercises available through her website.[22] These movements can be used to create choreography that is as complex as ballet or as simple as ten minutes a day exercises. It seems that, if we want our children to learn without the great effort it takes to get around learning difficulties, we need to get them moving. We expect children to sit still for hours and focus, but this may be the most counter-productive thing for them.

Developing the cerebellum is key to improvement in learning difficulties, and I have seen some remarkable changes in people who had serious ready, balance, focus and writing problems through the therapies we used at Hallowell's center. All of the sensory motor/balance based therapies note the connection between certain types of exercise or auditory stimulation and the cerebellum. More study needs to be made, but the data that has been uncovered indicates that neurogenesis, or the development of new brain pathways, can be assisted by movement from childhood all the way into our 90s. This is good news to those who have had their development arrested by sedentary ways if they will take the cure of increasing their activity for their brain's sake.

---

21. Jensen, "Teaching with the Brain in Mind."

22. Gilbert, "Brain Dance."

Dr. Carla Hannaford who wrote *Smart Moves: Why Learning Is Not All in Your Head*,[23] and Dr. John Ratey, author of *Spark*,[24] whom I had the pleasure of meeting, both agree that neurological problems and subsequently learning difficulties can be improved by movement. These give you the precise biochemistry released by movement and offer some enlightening statistics.

Ratey postulates that brain development and the brain are inextricably intertwined and he cites the sea slug (a creature that eats its own brain as soon as it attaches to a rock because it knows it will never move again and hence does not need it). He explains physical activity is imperative to the wellness of the brain.

Similarly, the Chinese use Tai Chi (a form of balance exercise) in groups before class and even before work at industrial, corporate, and university levels to increase productivity, while many of us here in the US turn to the use of some sort of stimulant like coffee, despite its side effects of anxiety and sleeplessness.[25]

Forest Schools also use music to improve learning, and part of what I did at Hallowell's center involved the Integrated Listening Program inspired by Dr. Alfred Tomatis,[26] a French Ortho-laryngologist and author of the acclaimed *The Voice and the Ear*. In the 1950s, he discovered the remarkable effects of gated music on the remediation of learning problems. Listening to music (some kinds more than others) stimulates development in the acoustic and proprioceptive mechanisms of the ear, which constitute a direct line to the cerebellum and promote development and healing. Playing music does even more as the movement of the fingers along with the stimulation of the inner ear (as in singing and dancing) activate more centers of the brain, causing musicians to have more neurological connections between left and right brain than others do. Dyslexics have fewer connections, but those can be grown with the right kind of stimulation.[27]

Those who have the means can avail themselves of much that will help their learning disabilities. The poor have little to nothing. As public schools

23. Hannaford, *Smart Why Learning Is Not All in Your Head*.

24. Ratey, *Spark*.

25. "Dr. Ge Wu who teaches in the areas of biomechanics, movement science, kinesiology, evidence-based practice, and research methods at the University of Vermont has done extensive research connecting increased productivity and Tai Chi." Wu, "Biomechanical Analysis of Tai Chi Quan Movement."

26. Tomatis, *The Voice and the Ear*.

27. Miller, "Music Builds Bridges in the Brain."

are undermined and ignored by budgets, less may be given to the average student and much less to the learning disabled. Kids with difficulties learn better in smaller classes and the overcrowding due to lack of funds and teachers is another problem undermining them. Private schools do not usually have the means to offer anything to special learners. Specialized schools are very expensive. Lack of effective programs is a real problem that is getting worst and the connection between criminal activity and learning disability is too large to ignore.

After my time with the wealthy who could afford these therapies, I returned to serving the poor. I now work with the homeless and teach them how to manage the system to get off the streets in housing and stay sober. The wealthy have a sense of entitlement. They can walk into any place and feel they have a right to services and quality treatment. The poor have been taught they have a right to nothing, hence they have only their pain and their anger, and they feel they are not entitled so they will suffer, or they will steal what they need. We have to show the poor they are human first, then we can teach them what they are entitled as humans to learn and what will move them forward in their lives. The American dream has been proven to be more fantasy than fact, but that never stopped real heroes from emerging from the ranks of the lowly. Jesus was poor, and he changed the world. We must teach those who are down and out they that they have something to offer humanity too. We can also learn from them, and we must let them know this.

Whatever we teach, if we do not include a lesson that helps a student learn how to live a better life, we might as well hang up our credentials and go home. They can learn facts on the internet. They can only learn how to live from other human beings who themselves are living lives worth living! Technology may well take your job someday, but it can never take away your power to teach if you know this fact: Only life begets life.

Poverty is a great drawback to education. Where those with means help their children, often those who are poor must work two jobs to survive and at the same time support their own aging parents. Who has time for school? Still, greatness is found in the ranks of the poor and the learning impaired that many will never hear of. My daughter is an artist and business manager for a high-end salon on Newbury Street in Boston and she acquired this job through a blessed accident. She is also dyslexic. I have asked her if she would wave away her disability if she could. She answered definitively, "NO!" Feeling her creativity is somehow tied to her "problem," she said, "Think of all the amazing people with problems who have come out in history. The world may not have appreciated them the way they should, but it would be a terrible place without them." I have to agree. We as teachers must help them find their place of genius. Then they will flourish instead of flounder.

Natives do not trust people who give them things (even with good intentions) but do not befriend them. Friendship justifies exchanging of gifts but not hit and run acquaintance. When I was in high school, I was a bit shell-shocked by all I had experienced in the ghetto. I took it out on my guidance counselor who was a caring person. I jumped on her desk one day and made a scene. She had me sent to the remedial counselor Don Wald. I had heard about him and was scared, because Don was 300 pounds of muscle, with a bald head and a Fu Man Chu beard. I learned a lot with him, because he became a friend. I think I would not have made it without a friend like that. When we teach, we have to be a friend.

Remember the teaching imperative to share life, while teaching in a content creatively. Remember every child learns differently. Earn respect by giving respect and modeling it, remembering your culture is not the only one that is important. Use your subject to teach your students life's lessons to which they can relate. Discover and tell the stories that hide in every subject. History rightly told should reveal to them secrets of their own past. Show them why they need everything you teach them. Effective education instructs the body, mind, and spirit. Keep your students curious; keep them moving. Be a bridge to their better life.

Chapter Two

Modeling Success in the Inner-City Classroom from a Christian Perspective

GEMMA WENGER

WHEN I WAS FIRST asked to write a chapter on teaching English Language Learners in the inner city, my very first thought was what do I have to offer? I know there are experts out there who have written books on the subject, who have done extensive research, and who have created curricula. How do I know this? Because I have been trained in their research and applied their strategies in the inner city with English Language Learners (ELLs) and Standard English Learners (SELs) over a twenty-five-year period. Then I thought about it very carefully. Yes, I do have something to offer. I have personal experience of successes as well as failures in the second largest school district in the United States enrolling the largest number of Title I at-risk English Language Learners (ELLs) and Standard English Learners (SELs) in numerous lower socio-economic—impoverished, gang—infested neighborhoods. How many others can say that they were a literacy coach who trained teachers how to teach English Language Arts in South Los Angeles just a few blocks from where Rodney King was attacked? How many others have worked in two different project-feeder schools in Watts, namely Nickerson Gardens and Jordan Downs, and comforted children the day after a massive gang shooting in the Jordan Downs projects as an assistant principal whose main focus was intervention for the 70% Hispanic ELL students and the 30% African American SELs? How many others can say they were bridge coordinators over special education at one of *the*, if not *the*, lowest performing middle schools in the district wherein the Special Education children consisting of ELLs and SELs made a 23-point gain on the Academic Performing Index (API) while every other subgroup went down? I am blessed when I think about the fact that our Special Education teaching actually brought up the school's API as a whole. This is the school where I recall sitting in my office and looking out my window at eight police cars hastily rolling up to the house across the street. Six officers then got out with guns drawn and stealthily approached the house from the front while some went around the back. At that point, I vacated my desk and chair and squatted beneath the windowsill, peering out as this dangerous turn of events unfolded. I now know exactly what it looks like when police approach a house with guns drawn. If you ask me, I will do a fantastic imitation for you. I might look a little Charlie's Angelsesque, but I can laugh about it now. As we teachers always say, "Just the community activities that one encounters all in a day's work." These types of experiences, though, helped me understand what the children live with every day. Who else can say that they were at six Program Improvement (PI) schools as a Literacy Coach, Categorical Program Advisor, and Assistant Principal over Intervention, Special Education, and General Education where students made massive gains through targeted instruction and intervention? Who else can say that they worked as an Assistant Principal in Special Education both in the affluent Bel Air School that she attended as a child and in Watts and South Los Angeles. I have had all those actual experiences and those points of reference. Lastly, who can say that they grew up with a Harvard Law school-educated father and a food stylist television personality, inventor, and author for a mother? In this case, only me! Therefore, I feel I am qualified. From my experience, I can tell you what works and what does not work in teaching English Language Arts and English to the ELL children of the inner city because I have lived it and have seen the data support effective practices.

I also come with the background of a lifetime of serving in the ministry as a Christian pastor, evangelist, singer, television and radio producer, and author. I accepted Jesus in my heart when I was four years old and I was baptized in the Holy Spirit with the evidence of speaking in tongues at nine years of age. My entire life has been surrendered to the Lord with a strong desire to serve Him and to win souls for the kingdom of heaven. What does this have to do with empowering Christian educators in the classroom? I served God in the ministry while at the same time working in the field of education. Paul made tents for a season. I too have had my season of working in the secular world to meet my financial obligations. I must say, though, that the professional trainings programs that I was afforded by the school system over the years have made me a stronger leader, a more collaborative team member, a more knowledgeable assessor of the world's systems and of the legal rights of our English Language Learners and our students with disabilities. I transferred the knowledge and skills that I gained as a school site administrator into successfully working with people in the ministry. There are certain effective ways to handle situations that work. Strong prayers and a stellar character alone will not manage your class or teach your ELLs core content. The course of nature runs on certain principles of action or doing. If you utilize research-based strategies that have shown proven results with your intuition gained from your faith in the Lord, then you will excel completely. You cannot have faith alone without effective instructional and behavioral techniques, and effective teaching strategies without faith will not take your students completely where they need to go.

Another very important component that I must add to my analysis of an effective Christian teacher is that, the more healed we are spiritually, mentally, and emotionally, the better teachers we will be for all our students including our ELLs. My mom was very verbally abusive among other things, and I was stripped of much of my self-esteem when I was a child. As a result, I was very weak in the area of disciplining children. My inferiority complex and lack of confidence prevented me from feeling worthy that children should behave in the manner in which I wanted them to behave. My natural tendency was to let them do what they wanted, and I went along with their program. A good teacher decides what she wants students to do and then trains them to do just that through a variety of strategies and accommodations. Too many parents are following their children around and complying with their child's requests instead of the child doing what the parents' desire. As the Lord healed my character, my confidence grew, and I demanded respect. Students quickly fell into line due to the clear behavioral expectations with which I provided them. The strength of my character showed through as I dealt with children, and they knew that they had to give me their best because I would accept nothing less. My own healed spirit caused me to be able to encourage children as well as adults to reach their highest potential instead of settling for what they managed to give me.

I was able to counsel teachers in such a way that they could achieve the next level in their teaching and educational pedagogy.

As a UCLA graduate with a BA in Economics and as brand-new teacher fresh out of Cal State Northridge's (CSUN) two-year teaching credential program, I needed to find a full time elementary school teaching position. I did just that. I never could have imagined the path that the first position I chose would lead me. My personal philosophy was to say yes to the first opportunity that came along, and I did just that. I became a first grade teacher for twenty-three inquisitive ELLs and SELs in the inner city where the prostitutes walked the street outside, and the drug dealer who drove the white Mercedes lived in the house across the way from my classroom. I had never before heard people say, "you is" or "that's mines" or "I be." I learned quickly that the inner city had no anthologies or workbooks, no curriculum, and they expected children to share scissors among themselves as well as between classrooms. As a first-year teacher, I discovered my class was termed by the previous veteran kinder teacher as the worst class that she had ever had. Additionally, the veteran teachers had taken all the books before I arrived, and, when they were finally passed down to me after they were finished with them, my students were already far behind. I remember when Jovanny opened his antiquated English Language Arts book to read and all the pages flew out like a fan. He thought it was funny, but I only wanted to cry.

I had no formal tests to measure my students' progress. I had no idea how to read the miniscule print on the California Standards chart that had been placed on my wall by the prior teacher that encompassed everything students needed to know from grades K-12. I lacked a total understanding of behavior management since I had always tried to be the perfect student, always did the right thing, and only ever got in trouble for talking twice in my entire educational career. I couldn't understand why these children didn't behave on their own cognizance. I had no understanding of positive and negative behavior reinforcement, the use of clear expectations to support classroom management, social skills training, or what an individual Behavior Support Plan (BSP) was. Growing up, I just did what was expected and never received a reward. I always did my homework, but these children rarely returned their homework. One of my greatest challenges was figuring out how to "make" these children do their homework.

Teachers from affluent neighborhoods don't realize that the teaching style with which they grew up is not adequate when teaching ELLs. The teaching strategies that teachers use to teach middle and upper class students will not produce the same results with your lower socioeconomic ELLs. I have seen those teachers whose scores were high with a certain group of students plummet when they were put with lower performing ELLs and SELs. As a new teacher working with ELLs, I never realized that the students didn't understand every word that I was saying. It never occurred to me that I needed to do something different. I was a conscientious, well-prepared teacher, yet I did not have the full understanding that I needed to use specific strategies to support the needs of ELLs. I taught them just like I would teach any native English-speakers. Without books, curricula, data to monitor progress, an understanding of research-based ELL strategies, little understanding of Special Education accommodations and supports, and a serious need to unpack the standards, I have no idea how I made it through the first year. Basically, I visited the closest teacher supply store and reproduced ditto after ditto—although I had to pay for my own dittos because the principal didn't provide us with copies either!

After I endured four years of teaching in a school where the current principal had been ousted from a prior school due to parent protest for what I would call "sheer insanity," the district provided a new principal who had an understanding of how to support teachers. One thing the new principal did was to allow every teacher access to the supply room to do away with what she considered a "hoarding philosophy." Teachers had literally been hoarding supplies. There actually was no shortage of supplies, just a refusal by the administration to share. Walking by the supply room guarded by a teacher's aide, I could see it was well stocked, which again made me ask myself: why did I have nothing? It is interesting to note that people would erroneously think that because this school was located in a lower socioeconomic neighborhood that is the reason why we lacked supplies and books. That was not the case! Schools with targeted student populations and greater needs are afforded more finances by the state and Federal government through special categorical funding. Human mismanagement and lack of priorities is what prevents the financial benefits from reaching the students. It also has to do with parent involvement. Parents in upper class neighborhoods let their voice be known, whereas the parents of your ELLs might feel inadequate in their ability to communicate in English, tend to go with the flow, trust the powers that be, and feel grateful for whatever they receive. There is a general lack of accountability to parents in some lower socioeconomic settings for the management and disbursement of school funds.

Under the new principal, I was chosen to be the Literacy Coach who was trained to work with teachers on how to teach English Language Arts to ELLs and SELs utilizing the Cognitive Coaching method. Math was generally easier for our ELLs and SELs, and they seemed to score better on the math tests. We adopted a reform program for English Language Arts instruction. It was amazing! That year standardized test scores increased as well as in all the ensuing years that I was at that school. What strategies did this program use that were so magical? Since then, these strategies have become commonplace in most programs that target ELLs and SELs. These strategies work for all students, but I have found that teachers of high performing students sometimes skip the basics. Unfortunately, when that occurs, if your once high performing child begins to flounder or need more support, neither the teacher nor the child has any basic interventions to which to revert.

In the early literacy program, phonemic awareness was emphasized. I had never heard of the oral and aural activity of breaking words up into sound parts (segmenting) and then blending them back together. Students were trained to hear individual sounds and play games with those sounds in words. Those sounds were then connected to letters and students began to spell and decode. Sound spelling cards were introduced which no longer emphasized, as in former days, one letter per sound but rather a myriad of spellings for one sound. Signals were also included to indicate where these types of spellings occur in words, for example, at the beginning or the end of words. Fun songs and choruses were developed to remember the spelling patterns and associations among the names of the cards, sounds of the cards, and spellings of the cards. Phonemic awareness is specifically beneficial for ELLs since they learn to read their own native language through partitioning words into syllables. Singing and chants are especially helpful for the Standard English Learner. Utilizing a rap song or popular top 40 song is a Culturally Relevant and Responsive strategy to target your SELs who are very responsive to music and performance opportunities. I included a student performance component to Back-to-School night, and the once desolate, morgue-like atmosphere due to lack of parent participation completely changed. African-American and Latino/a parent attendance increased dramatically. All parents want to see their children perform, but, in this multicultural environment, it proved especially effective to encourage parent attendance.

A very interesting point that I would like to make is that generally the middle-class child arrives in kindergarten with many pretaught skills such as letter recognition, sound-symbol association, and the ability to decode some simple consonant-vowel-consonant words. They generally know how to count and can name the parts of the body. Their oral language development, concept development, and vocabulary far exceed that of the ELL student. Because of this, the teacher does not feel the need to engage students in these basic building blocks of literacy instruction and moves forward into the actual decoding and engagement of text. If you have a mix of ELLs and high performing students in your class, your ELLs do not receive the early literacy instruction that they need if you have skipped these foundational building blocks necessary for the ELL learner to learn. It is imperative that the teacher be aware of this and design small group instruction to meet the individual needs of all her students, including ELLs.

Whole group direct instruction lessons need to be scaffolded to meet the needs of the ELLs. Such students need frequent prompts incorporated within the whole group lesson to refer them to the Sound Spelling cards in order to review the sounds and spellings in words for purposes of reading, writing, spelling, and dictation. These strategies can also be called "intervention strategies." Students can be referred to a specific set of tools to utilize when they are faced with challenging tasks. An interesting point to note is that your native English speakers (excluding your SELs) and high performing children don't have this set of tools because past teachers generally skipped over these skills initially. The teacher felt they didn't need this foundation because the students come into kindergarten already performing at a high level. He/She may not have even bothered posting the Sound Spelling cards, thus, when students flounder later on, they have no educational intervention supports. If this is the case and you have ELL learners mixed together with your native English speakers, your ELLs are at a decided disadvantage. Your ELLs must engage in these strategies in order to access the curriculum. A teacher is often thinking that "most" of the class is meeting grade-level standards and therefore he/she is a good teacher. Unfortunately, the mentality that, if "most" of your students are doing well, then you have done your job, falls far short when you are dealing with ELLs, SELs, and Special Education (SPED) students. I have seen the scenario whereby Spanish ELLs are attending an upper socioeconomic school because their parent works in the neighborhood and they have been granted attendance to the school on a work permit. Those students have a right to access the curriculum, and, thus, their teachers have an obligation to teach ELL strategies in their classroom whether in a whole or small group setting.

The modern-day teacher must differentiate instruction to meet the needs of all students ELLs, SELs, SPEDs, lower performing, and gifted students alike. This involves more preparation on the part of the teacher and a greater understanding of instructional strategies that directly address unique individual needs. It involves an awareness of incorporating supports into the direct instruction lesson as well as setting up small group instruction based on students' similar needs. It entails a strong working knowledge of Tier 1, Tier 2, and Tier 3 intervention strategies. Once you have set up the classroom to attend to the needs of your ELLs, you are ready to decide what strategies are most effective and where they will fall in the continuum of Tiered strategies.

Tier 1 intervention strategies are the teaching techniques that the teacher includes in her whole group direct instruction lesson. Tier 2 strategies are the in-class small group or individualized instructional supports. Tier 3 strategies are any interventions that happen outside of the classroom, which are likely, such as summer school, after school intervention, a pull-out program from class, or Saturday school. An especially effective Tier 1 intervention for ELLs is the pre-teach. Any concept can be pre-taught to a small group of students before it is addressed to the entire group. In this way, ELLs are exposed to the learning prior to its formal introduction to the class as a whole. They are receiving multiple exposures to concepts and vocabulary which may be completely new to them, while it is likely that their native English-speaking counterparts may be more familiar with them. In this way, vocabulary and concept development, which are the weaknesses of ELLs, due to the very fact that they are Limited English Proficient (LEP), can be reinforced over multiple exposures. For example, an intervention for vocabulary development would involve creating a small group of ELLs and pre-teaching them the vocabulary that will be used in the English Language Arts Anthology or the science or Social Studies lesson. In this way, they have a basic initial understanding of the concepts and can further build on their knowledge base during whole group instruction. The utilization of a Word Wall is an effective strategy to teach vocabulary and concepts, and the Word Wall can later be used as a center to reinforce learning during

Independent Work Time (IWT). In the same way, the re-teach is small group instruction after instructing the formal lesson for those ELL students to whom the teacher may want to re-teach the material just taught. A quick comprehension check will help her decide who needs further support in the re-teach group. After the teacher has determined the level of understanding, she can create groupings based on need for that specific lesson.

It is important to understand that groupings are not homogeneous but rather heterogeneous. Rather than keeping the same children in the "low" group or the "high" group all the time, what is important is to look at which students need extra help on the various skills taught for that particular lesson. Students who don't need help don't have a group, while the others are placed in the group based on their need to acquire a certain skill. You may have certain ELLs in your group for one skill, but they may have caught on quickly and thus don't need extra help for the next skill. This type of intervention support involves frequent formal and informal data monitoring and comprehension checks by the teacher to determine where the gaps in understanding occur.

Dual language classes are basically teaching ELLs grade level content in Spanish while they are learning English. There is a minimum of English taught, and the focus is building and strengthening the home language as well as increasing content area knowledge. Data have shown that students who are strong in their home language grasp English more quickly. They are taught in their home language with which they are familiar so as to allow them access to the grade-level curriculum in Spanish and not miss out on that content while they are learning English. Once they catch up in their English skills, then students can learn the core content areas in English. The model that was used at my schools was as follows: In kindergarten, the students were taught 90% in Spanish and 10% in English. In first grade, students were taught 80% in Spanish and 20% in English. Then, in second grade, the students were utilizing Spanish 70% of the time and English 30%. Each successive grade increased the English by 10% and decreased the Spanish by 10%.

Based on my experience, I recognize this model sounds good on paper, yet the reality is a bit different. There are external factors which are not taken into consideration. For example, many ELLs are what we called "non nons." They aren't proficient in English nor are they proficient in Spanish. Non nons did not do well in the dual language program. It takes great skill to learn two languages. That is what they are essentially doing.

Their Spanish language and vocabulary skills are so limited that they have to be taught Spanish and their English skills are virtually nonexistent. Some ELLs only have the cognitive ability and processing skills to focus on one language at a time. They could possibly be an unidentified Special Education student. If they are going to learn a language, it is best to teach them English first instead of teaching them Spanish, in which they sorely lack proficiency, in order for them to learn English. Students who were not doing well in the Dual Language program were removed to classes taught in English with primary language support, English Language Development (ELD) and Specifically Designed Academic Instruction in English strategies (SDAIE), and 60 minutes of ELD instruction per day.

With Spanish being taught for most of the day in the early grades in the Dual Language Program and by fifth grade being taught fifty % of the time, class time provides a relatively small amount of exposure to English. English grammar, spelling patterns, vocabulary, and sentence structure are so complex in nature that even the most precocious ELLs need to have more time and experience with the material. Children catch on to and use language more quickly than do adults, and thus it is important that learning the English language be a priority without sacrificing grade level content. Primary language supports, English Language Development strategies and Specifically Designed Academic Instruction in English, have been shown to be sufficient in helping ELLs understand material taught in English. One bright African-American (Standard English Learner) from Watts was placed in a dual language program. After five years with the program, he was removed in his fourth grade year because he wasn't meeting grade level standards. His Spanish was sorely lacking and he spoke the African American Language (AAL) at home.

His grammatical sentence structures went unchanged. The program had failed him since he wasn't able to meet grade level standards in English Language Arts as he moved through successive grade levels.

As academic benchmarks increased in difficulty with each successive grade, the Dual Language program was not able to address the increased rigor of the standards and the typical results were students falling behind. The Dual Language program provides far too much Spanish language instruction to the point that it teaches, refines, and develops the student's Spanish language but doesn't expose them to enough English content to meet grade level standards. It is also targeting the best and the brightest of the ELLs, and those who cannot meet benchmarks are removed from the program. With the disenrollment of students from the Dual Language program who are not meeting benchmarks, the success of the program on data charts increases exponentially. But is it truly indicative of what is really happening in the classroom?

The Dual Language program clearly addresses those whose primary language is Spanish. What about those whose home language is Armenian, Korean, or Russian just to name a few of the types of second language learners that I have worked with in my educational career? It is impossible to provide Dual Language programs in all those languages, but, due to the large number of Spanish-speaking children, there are enough students to fill up an entire classroom with ELLs and parents are encouraged to enroll their children in this model with the strong enticement that their child will learn Spanish as well as English. Again, the Dual Language model heavily supports Spanish language acquisition and refinement for your top students who come in with a strong language base but does not provide enough exposure to the English language and all its intricacies. It does not address those students who test as non-Spanish speakers (not proficient in Spanish) and non-English speakers (not proficient in English) or, as I noted, those who are known as the "non nons." Those students need to be taught in English with ELD, SDAIE and primary language supports since they have a limited Spanish language foundation.

With the Lau v. Nichols (1974) Supreme Court decision, it was determined, "There is no equality of treatment by merely providing students with the same facilities, textbooks, teachers, and curriculum: for students who do not understand English are effectively foreclosed from any meaningful education . . . . we know that those who do not understand English are certain to find their classroom experiences wholly incomprehensible and in no way meaningful." The support models in which these ELLs participate are grouped into The Master Plan. The Master Plan provides various models that aid ELLs in learning English but at the same time accessing the grade level content. The Master Plan includes the following models:

1. Structured English Immersion

2. Transitional Bilingual Education

3. Maintenance Bilingual Education

4. Mainstream English Program

5. Dual Language Two-Way Immersion program

Structured English Immersion (SEI) focuses on the lower level ELLs acquiring English language proficiency and access to grade-level instruction via differentiated instruction and support. It utilizes English Language Development (ELD), Specifically Designed Academic Instruction in English (SDAIE), and primary language support.

The Mainstream Program focuses on the advanced ELLs: those who have been reclassified as proficient English Learners (RFEPS), Initially Fluent English Proficient Students (IFEPS), as well as English Only (EO) students. The goal is to acquire English language proficiency and master grade level instruction through ELD and SDAIE strategies as well as primary language support.

Transitional Bilingual Education involves acquiring English language proficiency and grade-level academic content through a combination of core content instruction via primary language, ELD, and differentiated instruction in English.

The Maintenance Bilingual Education program allows ELLs to acquire language proficiency and academic achievement in two languages: English and the students' primary language.

The Dual Language Two-Way Immersion supports students in acquiring language proficiency and academic achievement in two languages: English and the target language, as well as positive cross-cultural competencies for ELLs and English-proficient students.

If the focus is English language acquisition and grade-level content mastery, the most effective models are Structured English Immersion (SEI) and The Mainstream Program. The newest influx of ELLs to the inner city are coming from backgrounds wherein literacy, language, and vocabulary skills are at a minimum. They know so little of their own native language that there is no point in teaching them Spanish in order to learn English, although making connections with the limited background knowledge and experiences that they do have in Spanish will support learning. Teaching them first in Spanish to learn English distracts them from the ultimate goal of learning and becoming proficient in English. As a UCLA undergraduate student, I took Spanish, French, and German. I love languages and am completely in favor of students being multilingual, but, in the inner city, it is important to prioritize and not overwhelm the students who have minimal Spanish language skills by trying to actually teach them two languages. Families truly want their Spanish language preserved, but, cognitively, students are finding it difficult to learn two languages at the elementary level.

That leads me to the benefits of providing ELD and SDAIE support along with primary language support coupled with academic content instruction in English.

The goal of ELD instruction is defined by the ELD standards. Content learning is a by-product of learning English. It utilizes rich content through grade-appropriate text and teacher delivery, differentiated according to ELD levels. ELD is taught for 60 minutes per day in elementary school to increase English vocabulary, concept development, and sentence structure just to name a few skills. In my experience, ELD instruction is most effective when it correlates to the English Language Arts curriculum as well as the Science and Social Studies curriculum. When ELD and ELA themes coincide, students learn. Sadly, there is not enough time in the day to devote to ELD instruction, science, Social Studies, expository text, etc. separately, therefore, when ELA and ELD are taught within the context of and connected to the other content areas, you achieve two goals with one combined effort. You develop English skills and content knowledge.

The goal of SDAIE instruction is to teach grade level content defined by grade level standards and framework. Learning the English language is a by-product of learning content. Instruction in English can include primary language support and access to the core curriculum through intentionally planned scaffolds according to ELD levels. SDAIE is a methodology or a set of specific strategies designed to make instruction comprehensible and grade-level content accessible for English Language Learners (ELLs). There are four key elements essential to SDAIE instruction. The first element is content. Teachers need to determine key concepts and skills, design lesson objectives that focus on specific concepts and specific language, use district and state adopted grade-level material, and choose ancillary texts and other materials that will help clarify the content.

The second element is making connections, building bridges between what is to be learned and what students already know. Factors to be taken into consideration are previous content learning; processes such as think-pair-share and skills learned, such as outlining; utilizing personal experiences by selecting culturally responsive examples from the student's life to illustrate key concepts and organizing lessons that build on previous knowledge.

The third element of SDAIE is comprehensibility. Teachers need to combine visual cues such as pictures, diagrams with verbal and written communication; make one-to-one correspondence between spoken and written concepts and the visual cue; control range and diversity of vocabulary, for example, the use of idiomatic expressions which are one of the most difficult concepts for ELLs to grasp; repeat new key words in different concepts and chart them and check frequently for comprehension.

The fourth element is interaction. This element involves using a variety of student groupings, using modeling and sentence frames to scaffold academic language development, ensuring that students use targeted academic language, and asking many and varied questions at all different levels of Blooms Taxonomy or the Depth of Knowledge Levels.

ELD and SDAIE share many different characteristics, such as providing a linguistic and conceptual context for all instruction, tapping into prior knowledge and building background, providing many opportunities to practice and apply new learning, and using realia, visuals, graphic organizers, and thinking maps. When ELD and SDAIE strategies are used systematically and with fidelity, your ELLs learn.

One tried and true expression of my mentor was "good teaching is good teaching." Many of the strategies that I have previously mentioned, on which I have only touched the surface, though specifically designated targeted instruction for ELLs, will, in all honesty, support all students. Every student responds to exciting hands-on lessons that use visuals and graphic organizers to reinforce difficult concepts. Who doesn't love a good song, kinesthetic activity, or cooperative group activity? The use of Discussion and Participation protocols are some of my absolutely favorite strategies and are especially effective in allowing students to participate in new and innovative ways in the lesson. Rather than always being talked "at" by the teacher, they are given opportunities to learn through participation. I remember training Teach For America teachers attending a summer program in Watts who later went out into the most needy communities, using these strategies. They loved them! Students that I previously taught were elated when they were called to small group instruction with the teacher. Their attention and engagement increased exponentially, and their effort went off the charts. That specifically designed special small group attention aimed at meeting their identified need encouraged them to try harder. So many of our ELLs and SELs lack a positive home environment and respond to individual encouragement and personal attention. Utilizing small group, differentiated, scaffolded instruction to meet the needs of all learners, including your gifted students, is a necessary and essential routine for all classroom teachers.

As a Christian educator knowledgeable in Christian biblical principles who was asking God to give me wisdom in negotiating the task before me, I realized, when I began, that I had so much practical knowledge to gain in working in a lower socio-economic multi-cultural environment. The amount of academic verbal output between the ELLs and their more affluent native English-speaking counterparts was pronounced. I was not adequately trained or prepared to attempt to teach the ELLs at the "refined" level whereby students show the greatest academic gains. One of my principals who worked with me in a school located in an upper-class neighborhood which displayed top academic scores in the district asked me the following question, "Do you really think these teachers are any better than those in South Los Angeles who work with multicultural students?" I thought about it for a moment. I knew some were, but, as I continued to observe in classrooms, I realized that I was encountering a large percentage of excellent teachers as well as some mediocre ones. One thing that I did note was that the fax machine was constantly receiving fax after fax of teacher resumes. Everyone was applying to become a teacher there because they wanted to work at this high profile affluent elementary school. One teacher who applied and was hired had received the Walt Disney Teacher of the year award. He was an excellent teacher as you can imagine. On the other hand, the schools in South Los Angeles were making call after call to candidates who were refusing to come into those types of neighborhoods. I concluded that the "Bel Air" schools do have a greater choice of qualified personnel to choose from while the "South Los Angeles or Watts" schools have to choose from what is left and that affects the quality of education the students receive.

Another difference between the affluent versus the lower socioeconomic neighborhoods is that the parents may be less educated. Parents in the upper-class neighborhood provide strong language models at home, homework support, and tutoring. Parents of ELLs often feel that they cannot help their children at home academically due to their own limited knowledge. Because of this issue and a deep understanding on my part that parent involvement is an integral part of student success, I created Professional Developments for Spanish-speaking parents designed to train them how to support their children at home when they themselves do not have a strong grasp of the language or content material. One idea was to create a structured afterschool schedule whereby parents organized their time to include listening to their child read fluently in English or Spanish. Fluent reading in any language is still fluent reading. Parents can be trained to have students read a timed passage multiple times and graph progress. Parents can even read a text with their children in their native language and ask them "why" questions. Parents were also trained on the Sound Spelling and high frequency word cards and, as a result, were able to make a set of their own to review with their children at home. Just because parents don't know the language doesn't mean that they can't support their child's academic growth.

As a Christian educator, I needed to develop an understanding of the strategies and skills that worked with ELLs. Coming out of college and being told that the Latino people have a high transiency rate and go back and forth to their native country frequently is not going to encourage or empower me to teach ELLs. I was in no way prepared to instruct at the highest level to meet the specific needs of the ELLs even though I had a Cross-Cultural Language and Academic Development (CLAD) credential, and I was unprepared to deal with numerous behavior problems that occur at a much more intense level than what I was accustomed to expect. After much training, though, my attitude and actions turned around. I was able to develop strategies to support students in the classroom both behaviorally and academically. The key was incorporating the world's wisdom with my spiritual understanding and revelation from God. Today, I no longer am afraid to enter any class because the behaviors may be too intense for me to handle. I have been trained by the school district, by my own experiences, and by the voice of the Lord in a variety of strategies to deal successfully with any instructional or behavioral issue and afford all students an opportunity to learn, grow, and excel to become the best that they can be. Over time, as a teacher, I grew in experience and maturity. Most importantly, though, I had a strong walk with the Lord, and, through His inner healing process, I developed the confidence and strength that I needed to set a focus and ultimately achieve it. That person who at one time "just followed along" has now been described as having a "will of iron." I know God brought me through the most difficult teaching experiences of my life. It was by His grace that I am where I am today. I give Him all the glory and praise.

There is so much more to discuss on this topic, but that would fill numerous books. King Solomon wrote in Ecclesiastes 3:22, "So I saw that there is nothing better for a person than to enjoy their work, because that is their lot. For who can bring them to see what will happen after them?" (TNIV) God wants to bring us success as a direct result of our hard work and informed decision-making. When you see those ELLs grow and improve under your informed tutelage, you will rejoice that you are changing their lives through effective instructional strategies as well as changing the lives of multiple successive generations that you may never live to see. And you will be pleasing the God who created them and loves them.

Chapter Three

Strategies that are Scripturally Based for the Public-School Classroom

Julia Davis

INTRODUCTION

TEACHERS ARE CHALLENGED TO engage students personally and to manage classroom climate and instruction. The purpose of this chapter is to identify strategies that integrate knowledge and skills from educational experience and Scripture. As a teacher with over thirty years' experience teaching in New York, Maryland, and Washington DC inner city public schools, I have modified teaching techniques to the learning needs of "at risk" and "special education" and English Language Learning students. Here are some general guidelines to approach the teaching of these special students, but useful as well to any classroom population.

DEFINING TERMS OF CLASSROOM MANAGEMENT

"Classroom management refers to the wide variety of skills and techniques that teachers use to keep students organized, orderly, focused, attentive, on task, and academically productive during a *class.*"[1]

I will begin by defining the terms as I understand them. Techniques are ways of executing a specific task by employing a combination of known

---

1. The Glossary of Education Reform, "Classroom Management."

and unknown variables hopefully to achieve a successful end. Teaching is the ability to convey/transfer combinations of knowledge, information, and experience to impact change in thought behavior and disposition. As I teach, I adapt techniques to the uniqueness of the learner. I will discuss teacher preparation and expectations for students later in this chapter. The term at-risk has been bantered since the mid-20th century. I understand at-risk to mean being in danger of falling through society's fissures and holes due to lack of preparation, or not having the necessary safeguards and structures prevent being preyed upon due to vulnerability, to possessing only borderline survival skills. What does all that mean? The term "at—risk" is the perception that student vulnerability due to a lack of society or culturally accepted norms presupposes that student will precipitate into academic and, therefore, life nonsuccess. Students are lifelong learners making constant application toward advancement and productivity. Inner city schools are often learning monoliths subject to disintegration due to the lack of the life blood of the spiritual infusion of love for learning, sharing, and building community.

OPPORTUNITIES UNLIMITED REMEDIAL SERVICES (O.U.R.S.) CHILD DEVELOPMENT CENTER

"Teachers improve the most early in their careers. One study found that close to half of the teacher achievement returns to experience arise during the first few years of teaching."[2]

Before sharing some of my teaching strategies, I will address the personal outlook I required to sustain me mentally, physically and spiritually. First and foremost, I had to have a very strong faith in God and His ability to restore me on a daily basis because the outlook in the first classroom and child development center where I was employed as head teacher was very dismal. I was located in an area of the South Bronx New York, near a neighborhood called Fort Apache, known for extreme violence, robberies, garbage loaded streets, teenage moms, open alcoholic debris and a spirit of heaviness and sadness that hovered over the community. When I first arrived, I thought I had stepped into an old World War Two war zone that I had seen in old movies. Even the sky was dark hovering over the burnt-out store fronts and sad depressed looking people. I was glad to live with

2. Clotfelter, Ladd, and Vigdor, "How and Why Do Teacher Credentials Matter for Student Achievement?," line 6–9.

a missionary family in Peekskill, New York. The long ride home helped to revive me, so I could go back another day to see and care and teach the little children ages 2.6 months to 6 years old. Many of these children had to step over overdosed bodies to come to school at the O.U.R.S. Child Development Center. This center was started by a member of the community and a local minister and missionary Katherine Brooks.

The child care facility provided four meals a day, including hot breakfast, hot lunch, and snacks. Many times these children only had food at the center. We had to apply for federal funds for a hot foods program to hire a cook. The children's health care needs were met through a nurse (RN) who came to the center three times a week.

I learned the following classroom management skills while teaching at the O.U.R.S. Child Development Center that have become critical to my success as a teacher:

FIRST IMPRESSIONS

The concept of making a good first impression is Biblical. According to Titus 2:1 Christian teachers must conduct themselves "so that in every way they will make the teaching about God our Savior attractive." Making a good first impression as a teacher instills a very important group dynamic. A good impression holds the students' interest and makes them feel welcomed and fosters a sense of classroom security. I always dress respectfully in the classroom. A teacher must dress with authority even if it appears out of context in the classroom. Clothing and attitude speak loudly. Personal orderliness and structure speak of the teacher's professionalism and ability to answer and resolve real life questions.

You never get a second chance to make a first impression. Speaking clearly, making appropriate eye contact and smiling sincerely, listening actively, monitoring body language, being polite and courteous and positive, all contribute to a good first impression.

TAKING CARE OF YOURSELF SO THAT YOU CAN TAKE CARE OF YOUR STUDENTS

Maria Delaney has observed, "Pupils in school are very aware of the mental and physical state of their teachers. They seem to recognize the importance of well-being and stress management in learning. Do we?"[3] The first teaching strategy is to take care of yourself, so you can present a healthy positive attitude toward your teaching environment and to your students whether or not it is a first day or in a school war zone. Environment is mentioned first because you are your environment. I calm down and reduce stress by praying daily before class for myself and for my students as follows:

"I bow before the Father who made me, I bow before the Son who saved me, I bow before the spirit who guides me, In love and adoration, I give my lips, I give my heart, I give my strength, I bow and adore thee, Sacred Three, The Ever One, the Trinity. In Jesus Name Amen."[4]

"Dear Heavenly Father, I pray for a wall of protection today around my students to keep the enemy away and the bullies at bay. In Jesus Name, Amen." [5]

I remember not to sweat the small stuff by reciting Philippians 4:6, 7: *"Do not be anxious about anything, but in everything by prayer and supplication with thanksgiving let your requests be made known to God. And the peace of God, which surpasses all understanding, will guard your hearts and your minds in Christ Jesus."* If I am burnt out I rest in the Lord as Psalm 23:2-3: calls all Christians to lie down in green pastures as He leads us beside quiet waters and restores our souls guiding us in the paths of righteousness For His name's sake.

"In the same way, let your light shine before others, so that they may see your good works and give glory to your Father who is in heaven." Matthew 5:16 ESV

TEACHERS ARE ROLE MODELS

"A role model is a person who inspires and encourages us to strive for greatness, live to our fullest potential and see the best in ourselves. A role model is someone we admire and someone we aspire to be like."[6] The teacher's presence makes a statement about what the children can expect. Your very presence projects elements of order, security, and acceptance. Oftentimes the students' perception of the teacher is that, if she takes care about her-

---

3. Delaney, "Teacher Stress, Well-being and Stress Management: Taking Care of Yourself So That You Can Take Care of Your Students," lines 3–5.

4. Adam, "Adoration," *Poetic Celtic Prayers*, 9.

5. Pinterest, "Explore Belief Quotes, Prayer for Protection, and more!"

6. Teach, "Teachers Are Role Models," lines 1–5.

self, she will care about them and respect their differences. Demeanor and choice of words, ice breaker activities, class setting, visual and auditory sensory ambiance must exude joyful learning and restful time outs. As a teacher I model good cheer in spite of lack of classroom equipment and other enrichments. It's important to be creative. Recycle. Make "the dollar holler." Involve the parents and see what skills they have to contribute to their child's education.

'But all things should be done decently and in order." 1 Corinthians 14:40

EFFECTIVE USE OF STRUCTURE IN THE CLASSROOM

As a Christian teacher, I put order into school surroundings and routines that help the classroom to be more efficient and purposeful: "Structure and support go hand in hand with one another and therefore we discuss them as paired concepts. When a teacher is preparing the classroom activities he or she must also consider what the learners need in order to success-fully complete the task."[7] Providing and insisting on structure is extremely important for teachers vested staff and therapists, and other school staff as well as family caretakers. Structure is necessary for all learners to have because it provides constraints and restraints to many learners who have not learned the skill of inner control and delayed gratification. Teachers must model appropriate behavior within morally and socially acceptable standards and frameworks. Modulating the teacher's tone by using a voice level that is quiet but firm while interacting with students in structured and unstructured learning situations and opportunities is essential. Even when "off duty" so called teachers must portray an approachable demeanor, encouraging open for receiving appropriate behavior. These opportunities can represent themselves at supermarket, gas stations, amusement parks, houses of worship, while taking public transportations, dog walking etc. A teacher is a leader.

Howard Wills and colleagues observe: "A second classroom strategy that increases student opportunity to engage in appropriate behavior and aligns well within SW-PBIS (School-Wide Positive Behavioral Interventions and Supports) model is the explicit teaching and reinforcement of classroom rules and behavioral expectations. After implementing these

7. Best of Bilash, "Offering Structure and Support in the Language Classroom," lines 4–8.

strategies within the classroom setting teachers report fewer student problem behaviors, report using a higher ratio of praise to reprimands with students and report feeling less distracted by problematic behaviors and feel they have more time to teach."[8]

Structure gives a sense of security, and direction and promotes ownership of one's behavior, and strengthens a group concept and its common ground. Structure supports individual responsibility to maintain group cohesiveness. Structure with definitive rules provides a vehicle to reach group goals. Definitive group structures help individual students discover their own bent, strengths, and weaknesses.

"Train up a child in the way he should go, and even when he is old he will not depart from it." (Prov. 22:6)

CLASSROOM RULES

"Discipline problems in schools continue to be one of the greatest causes of concern for educators in schools today. The Bible, in Proverbs 22:6, commands, "Train up a child in the way he should go, and even when he is old he will not depart from it." This verse is a clear promise and direction from God. As such, it is not a coincidence that as prayer and the Bible are removed from schools, children are able to test the boundaries of their teachers and parents, which in turn leads to disciplinary challenges. As the training opportunities are removed, the discipline problems are increased. Many public opinion polls have cited discipline as a major problem in the schools."[9]

Scripturally based "Classroom Rules" are a way to bring knowledge of Christian principle into the public-school classroom without being 'politically incorrect'. My students begin each class by devising classroom principles. When students have written the *Classroom Rules* they are more apt to abide by them.

For example, "I am ready to be respectful and responsible and a good classroom citizen" reflects the values of Psalm 19:14,[10] Proverbs 18:24[11]

---

8. Wills, Iwaszuk, Kamps and Shumante, "CW–Fit: Group Contingency Effects Across the Day," 191.

9. MacMillan, "Imbedding Christian Values in the Public Education Setting," 1.

10. Psalm 19:14: "May these words of my mouth and this meditation of my heart be pleasing in your sight, LORD, my Rock and my Redeemer." (NIV)

11. Proverbs 18:24: "A man who has friends must himself be friendly, but there is a friend who sticks closer than a brother." (NIV)

and Mark 12:31.[12]"Listening without interrupting" describes the wisdom of Proverbs 18:2.[13] "Speaking without accusing" is a mandate of James 1:19.[14] "Answering without arguing" is an instruction of Proverbs 17:1.[15] Ephesians 4:15 outlines the importance of sharing.[16] "Forgiveness without retribution" is a mandate of Colossians 3:13.[17]

"Let no corrupting talk come out of your mouths, but only such as is good for building up, as fits the occasion, that it may give grace to those who hear." Ephesians 4:29 (ESV)

LANGUAGE

"We communicate with others all the time. But how good are we at it?"[18] As a teacher, I learn the jargon, the local vernacular, and I use it appropriately as the occasion arises to make a point without swearing or using abusive language. As a teacher, I never name-call or use poor speech. The teacher's language should give the student the opportunity to express and often defend themselves. As I teach, I model correct verbal communication. When a teacher thinks and speaks logically, she models rational sequential thinking for the student. Teachers, staff, and caretakers must model appropriate verbal responses when diffusing a situation, removing guilt or shame by using calming language. Modeling the correct use of language is important

12. Mark 12:31: "The second is this: 'Love your neighbor as yourself.' There is no commandment greater than these." (NIV)

13. Proverbs 18:2: "Fools find no pleasure in understanding, but delight in airing their own opinions." (NIV)

14. James 1:19: "My dear brothers and sisters, take note of this: Everyone should be quick to listen, slow to speak and slow to become angry." (NIV)

15. Proverbs 17:1: "It is better to eat a dry crust of bread in peace and quiet than to eat a big dinner in a house that is full of fighting." (NIRV)

16. Acts 2:42–47: "And they devoted themselves to the apostles' teaching and the fellowship, to the breaking of bread and the prayers. And awe5 came upon every soul, and many wonders and signs were being done through the apostles. And all who believed were together and had all things in common. And they were selling their possessions and belongings and distributing the proceeds to all, as any had need. And day by day, attending the temple together and breaking bread in their homes, they received their food with glad and generous hearts, praising God and having favor with all the people. And the Lord added to their number day by day those who were being saved."

17. Colossians 3; 13: "Bear with each other and forgive one another if any of you has a grievance against someone. Forgive as the Lord forgave you."

18. Ho, "The Importance of Effective Communication," 1.

to help students formulate language that helps them *save face*, stand up to bullies, be thoughtful and caring, be sensitive to needs and the feelings of others. What has this got to do with reading? Everything if it breaks the concept, idea, or notion that they can't learn, that they are stupid and can't think, and that English Language Learners and students with special needs can only get attention through negative behavior.

"Educators find more success in providing students with explicit instruction about classroom rules and behavioral expectations rather than temporarily or permanently removing the student from the learning environment. Research supports the use of a proactive method for addressing behavioral expectations and rules students routinely have difficulty following. These practices allow students who struggle greater opportunity to stay in the classroom and engage in appropriate behavior. While schools need a consistent, systematic response to unsafe and inappropriate behavior, research-based prevention and interventions—not zero tolerance policy—reduce disruptive and off-task behaviors of youth in schools."[19]

CONCLUSION

"Whatever your hand finds to do, do it with your might, for there is no work or thought or knowledge or wisdom in Sheol, to which you are going." Ecclesiastes 9:10 (ESV)

THE CRITICAL IMPORTANCE OF WELL-PREPARED
TEACHERS FOR STUDENT LEARNING AND ACHIEVEMENT

"Since teachers have the most direct, sustained contact with students and considerable control over what is taught and the climate for learning, improving teachers' knowledge, skill and dispositions through professional development is a critical step in improving student achievement."[20] Good teachers for English Language Learners, special needs students, but, honestly, for all students, need special training and skills, not simply a good general education. I have found in my years teaching, training, and modeling appropriate behavior in diverse learning settings, that the teacher's personal

19. Wills, Iwaszuk, Kamps, and Shumate, "CW-Fit: Group Contingency Effects across the Day," lines 23–29.

20. The National Academies, of Science, Engineering, Medicine, "The Critical Importance of Well-Prepared Teachers for Student Learning and Achievement," lines 12–16.

commitment to standards of excellence reflects many hours of preparation. Making a good first impression by taking care of yourself so that you can take care of your students; role modeling correct dress and demeanor in and out of the classroom, implementing the effective use of structure and modeling language that is constructive seem obvious strategies, but when they are not practiced the class degenerates and the students miss out.

Chapter Four

Instructing English Language Learners in a Secular College

JEAN A. DIMOCK

"Do not neglect to show hospitality to strangers, for by doing that
some have entertained angels without knowing it."
(Heb.13:2 NRSV)

"Be hospitable to one another without complaining"
(1 Pet.4:9 NRSV)

"The alien who resides with you shall be to you as the citizen
among you; you shall love the alien as yourself, for you were
aliens in the land of Egypt: I am the Lord your God."
(Lev.19:34 NRSV)

COLLEGE-AGE LEARNER

THE INFORMATION IN THIS chapter applies to teaching college students
who are English Language Learners (ELLs). While much included
here applies to teaching any age learner, some information may not apply
to every age level. At the same time, there is likely much that can be applied to younger ages that are not incorporated here.

Providing instruction in philosophy and psychology courses at a
community college in New Hampshire (part of the university system) has

provided some instinctual as well as practical realizations for teaching ELLs. We may think that classrooms including ELLs are mainly Latino and Latina students, but that is not always the case. Instructing classes that have informed this chapter include first generation students from all over the world: Ukraine, Russia, Iran, France, Viet Nam, and Ireland, to name only a few. Class sizes in this school never exceed 25 students, at least within the humanities and psychology departments.

Presented here is an exceptionally simple, practical methodology washed in the hospitality ingredients of *grace and good manners*; at the same time, this approach maintains a *professional* posture. Intentional approaches that may be helpful to English Language Learners are also helpful to those who are not.

SCRIPTURES

In the above Scriptures, we are exhorted to show hospitality to strangers and to do so without objecting or grumbling. Furthermore, we are to treat "aliens" as if they were not foreigners or strange to us, but we are to show them the same grace and openness of heart we show everyone else familiar to us.

Why are Scriptures related to hospitality offered here? How does hospitality relate to teaching and the classroom environment? How does a concept that is generally reserved for home and church life translate into the classroom, especially as it relates to teaching those whose primary language is not English? Can hospitality and professionalism live together? In a classroom setting, how is professionalism maintained if the underpinning of hospitality is incorporated?

APPROACH

Grace and Good Manners

When visitors enter our home, we help them feel comfortable and welcome. Such actions have the ability to translate into what an instructor tries to accomplish when working with students in a classroom setting. Instructors, to follow through with the concept of incorporating hospitality in their teaching environment, need to provide an attitude and deeds that help every student relax, inasmuch as that is in that instructor's power. Hospitality in the classroom comes in many forms, including assuring safety for each student and helping students succeed.

When an educator expresses honor for those students who choose to take college classes in the United States when their first language is not English, ELL students are more than appreciative. Outward and clear expressions of respect for ELLs in the class bring a countenance of thankfulness and relief every time. Doing so provides these students the surety that the instructor understands, to some degree, the challenges specific to those whose first language is one other than English. Doing so also provides a sense of safety.

Honoring the student also implies having an understanding of the student's native culture. If an instructor does not already have knowledge of a certain culture represented in the classroom, he or she can do a little research. Why does my Ukrainian student seem so suspicious? Why is this other ELL student always running late? Why won't my Asian student look me in the eye? Is the student exhibiting a personality trait or is there something within the native culture that explains these characteristics?

Throughout the entire semester, the students are reminded that one of the most important issues to the instructor is that she makes herself available to help each student if that help is requested. If a student is at risk of doing poorly, the instructor will intervene at the earliest indication of a problem. He or she is then directed to the appropriate help, which is available at the college in a department designed for this purpose.[1] Even the syllabus reflects the availability of the instructor as well as in-school academic help. The instructor also provides timely responses to emails, appointments before and after class, as well as appointments at other times convenient for the student.

To offer an environment that lowers stress, involves extending hospitality. That includes being available to help students and showing respect for English Language Learners, while recognizing that they have an added layer of challenges. At the same time, the standards that are expressed in the syllabus and in the first class are maintained.

---

1. The college has a large department of professionals that offers help to any student who needs tutoring, help with research papers, skills to help minimize learning challenges, help for ELLs, and more. In this college, the department is called CAPS, or Center for Academic Planning and Support.

PROFESSIONALISM

Before Class Begins

A part of helping the students feel welcome before they appear in class is the email the instructor sends to all the students about two weeks ahead of the first class. At that time, the syllabus is provided. There are many reasons for a comprehensive syllabus; one reason is to make sure all (or almost all) potential questions are addressed before the first class. There is a sense of security in knowing what is expected and what will have to be done during the term. Such information helps students feel more comfortable and secure coming into the first class. Not too long ago, one student made an amusing comment on his course evaluation at the end of the term's last class: "Your syllabus is the best cheat sheet anyone could ever have because everything is outlined and explained and there are no surprises. We know everything we have to do over the semester. All we have to do is do it."

First Class

Within the first 30 minutes of class, each student's first name should be committed to memory. Having no more than 25 students in a class makes this easier than initially presumed, even for someone who knows she was not good at remembering peoples' names. Notations by the instructor's class roster can help: "tattoo on wrist" or "lip ring" or "red hair" or . . . Make certain student names are pronounced correctly. Asking a student how to pronounce his or her name is wise if the pronunciation is not obvious, or you may ask the students if their names are being pronounced correctly. Do not settle for "that's good enough." If this present instructor's background had not included three years of French, pronouncing Guillaume's name may have been challenging. Guillaume was delighted his name was pronounced accurately. Also, in many cultures, the meaning of a name is significant. Honor the students by making sure each name is pronounced correctly.

One way an instructor can find out very early if students need help in a certain area is to have them fill out a form provided in the first class. Some questions on this form revolve around what the students believe will be their greatest challenge in the class; how the students feel they will do in the class, and what expectations the students have of the professor. The last question is the most important: "Is there anything you would like me to know about you that is not reflected in the answers to the questions above?" Many ELLs will let me know clearly that they have concerns related to the fact that English is not their first language. This opens the door for the instructor to find out what the specific concerns are and to offer help very early.

Many activities that occur in the first class may provide a sense of security. One is to explain expectations for the class and what is to be accomplished over the term. While all of the information needed for the class is in the approximately sixteen-page syllabus, providing an overview of its contents reinforces these requirements. What is true of children is often true for adults: there is a need for boundaries and a need for knowing what the boundaries are. Having this information not only provides a sense of security, but also provides a sense of freedom.

There are other concerns that are addressed in the first class that benefit everyone, especially English Language Learners. These include informing the students that every class will include a very short grammar lesson, information concerning how to study, the advisability of the use of colloquialisms, and an explanation of how one can determine how one learns best.

In each class throughout the semester, the instructor provides a grammar lesson that takes no more than five minutes in the beginning of class time. While the English Language Learner benefits from this exercise, so does everyone in the class. Common errors in grammar are addressed. When written research papers are submitted, the students keep in mind those common errors described in these mini-lessons, providing a better paper.

Many students enter college without knowing how to study or how to dissect a textbook chapter. Giving a five or ten-minute overview of a very successful study method called "SQ3R" is in order. Not every student will use it, in fact, few will, but for the few who do incorporate this study method, the instructor will hear expressions of thankfulness. This method is more work up-front but saves time in the long run. Briefly, SQ3R stands for: survey; question; read; rehearse; review. Survey the chapter to see what it is about; slide through the chapter again and write down questions revolving around headers and key words, leaving a space for the answer to each question; read the chapter, answering the questions as the chapter is read, and even adding questions where appropriate; rehearse the answers to the questions; then review to further encode the answers to the questions in the student's mind. Using SQ3R means students will know the material the night before the exam. Consequently, they will get a good night's sleep before the exam rather than pull an all-nighter.

Colloquialisms may be confusing to someone who is trying to master the English language. Using them is discouraged in the classroom and is not accepted in a formal research paper. A colloquialism is very informal language and may have different meanings in different areas of the same country and even from country to country (which is also true of hand gestures). For example, while living in Kentucky for a few years, this instructor, originally from the State of New York, took on the task of organizing Vacation Bible School in her church. When the young woman who often took care of the nursery during church service was asked if she would like to take care of the nursery during VBS, she replied, "I wouldn't care to." So, the response to her was, "Okay, no problem. I'll find someone who can." A look of disappointment washed over the poor woman's face. She then said, "No! I said I wouldn't care to!" After a short and ultimately amusing exchange, both of us discovered that "I wouldn't care to" means something very different in the north than it does in the south. In the north, it means, "I don't want to." In the south, at least in Kentucky, it means, "I want to."

Having each student discover whether she or he is a visual, auditory, or kinesthetic (tactile) learner also helps. In other words, do the students learn best through visual, auditory, or kinesthetic stimulation? If the students are unsure, have them take a simple and free online test to make that determination. Generally, visual and auditory learners are satisfied in a college classroom, but kinesthetic learners are not. Auditory learners are automatically taken care of because they learn best by hearing. To help visual learners, an outline is produced on the black board or white board as the lecture is produced, but it is incumbent upon students to take good notes to help with their own visual learning needs. Visual learners learn best by seeing. College level kinesthetic learners have the bulk of the responsibility to meet their tactile needs. Tactile learners take information in best by doing. First, these learners need to dress comfortably. Then, as the instructor describes in the first class, the tactile learner has the ability to change seats during the lecture, or get up and stretch, or even bring a bean bag seat for comfort and a change of view. Other students are asked to be understanding and not distracted. Ultimately, knowing one's learning style helps to adjust study habits outside the classroom.

In the first class, let the students know that, if there is a word they do not know or understand on a quiz, test, exam, or in a lecture, they need to ask. Every student needs to understand what is being communicated.

Ongoing Classes

Speak slowly and carefully when lecturing, giving instructions, or asking a question. When asking a question, wait to ask for a response to give all students time to think about their answer. Students whose first language is not English often need extra time to translate the question into their native language and then translate the answer back into English. Patience needs to reign if a student asks to have the question repeated. When this happens, remember not to speak more loudly unless they state they cannot hear you. Perhaps simpler words are needed for them to understand the question. At the same time, this instructor remembers what her granddaughter said about the ELLs in her school: when her Russian friend is trying to tell her something, she needs to wait patiently for what her friend is saying rather than try to help her with the response unless her friend asks for help.

Breaking up in small groups to accomplish a task helps those who are hesitant to contribute to a full classroom, whether a student is an introvert or an ELL. Doing so helps students engage with other students within a less intimidating environment. Pairing students to have conversation about a topic is just as helpful and even provides more encouragement for a reticent student to participate, as it takes at least two people to have a conversation. Students who will not participate in the larger classroom setting will nearly always participate in a small group; every student will participate when paired.

Outside Class

As mentioned above, students can meet with the instructor either before or after class, or through another special appointment if they have questions, concerns, or need more instruction. Outside of class time, students are also able to get any tutoring and other academic help they need from CAPS, also mentioned above.

SUCCESS

The goal for students is to give each the information and tools necessary so every one of them will have a full opportunity to meet with success. As a colleague once said, "There is a point where the instructor leaves off and the student begins." The instructor can provide everything the student needs, but, ultimately, the student is responsible for using the information provided and then picking up the tools and using them properly.

Give English Language Learners the opportunity of succeeding at the same level and requirements as the native-born students. Do not automatically assume they cannot perform at the same level with the same skills as those students whose first language is English. Perhaps some ELLs have become more acculturated or perhaps these students have been immersed in the English language and its idioms since they were "knee high to a grasshopper." Then there will be those whose command of the English language may be far less. At the first indication of a problem, find the help they need. Doing so is simple if there is a department in the school that addresses student challenges. Providentially, this instructor has those resources available.

CONCLUSION

At the basis of what is helpful to English Language Learners on the college level, according to this instructor's own experience, hospitality provides the foundation of every aspect of help given to the student. Scripture tells us to extend our hospitality to everyone, including strangers, and to do so without complaining. Being hospitable means extending grace and good manners. At the same time, instructors need to remain professional.

Showing all students respect is important. Remembering to honor ELLs by telling them there is great respect for them and their efforts when English is not their native language shows them that there is a certain amount of understanding related to their challenges. Honoring students means recognizing important characteristics about their culture so the instructor can better understand each student. Sometimes, identifying ELLs quickly comes through having them fill out a form in the first class, where an ELL will often explain where they might need extra help.

One way to provide a sense of security and even freedom is to have a very complete syllabus that is reviewed during and reinforced in the first class. Helping the students to study more effectively means reviewing a successful study method and helping the students assess how they learn. Quick and easy grammar lessons that include common mistakes in grammar help the students produce better writing.

Instructors who speak slowly and carefully and without the use of regional language when lecturing, or simply speaking to the class, have a much better chance of being understood by the ELLs. Allowing the ELLs a chance to respond without interrupting shows respect for these students' desire to contribute to the class. As already noted, breaking up into small groups early on to have conversations about class material is very helpful to the ELL (and introverts) because their hesitance to contribute decreases sooner, promoting greater opportunity for class participation and, therefore, participatory learning.

An instructor's availability to help students who need extra help is essential; many ELLs will take advantage of that help and the help of those who are put in place at a school to provide that extra help. Direct the students to the help they need at the first indication of need.

All of these suggestions are in place to meet the goal of providing the best opportunity for student success. There is nothing in any of these suggestions that violates professionalism. In fact, they can only raise the level of professionalism. As instructors put their best efforts forward, they will have the greatest opportunity of realizing the best possible result from their students.

Within the challenges and blessings associated with the teaching profession (and daily life, whatever that entails for each person), it is good to remember: "So whether you eat or drink, or whatever you do, do everything for the glory of God" (1 Cor. 10:31 NRSV). While everything mentioned here may seem like a lot of extra effort, giving students the best chance to succeed makes all the planning and doing very worthwhile.

Chapter Five

English as A Second Language (ESL)

Volunteer Programs in Churches and Public Libraries

MICHAEL AND JAN DEMPSEY

IMAGINE WITH US THE experience of a refugee. You are strapped in a plane, staring out the window and wondering if the hell you escaped could actually be preferable to this unknown future you are facing. You have never flown before, yet you must trust this aircraft to bring you and your family to a better life. You try to be brave, yet your resolve crumbles as everything that was once familiar, and comforting recedes into the distance. The homesickness and anguish are feelings that mirrors the plight of the mournful Psalmist who cried: "How can we sing the songs of the Lord while in a foreign land?" (Ps. 137:1-4 NIV).

In the 1970s and 1980s, The First Congregational Church of Revere, Massachusetts, sponsored 225 refugees and helped them adjust to life in the United States. A devout Christian couple, moved by the plight of refugees, donated their home to the church to serve as a waystation of hospitality for immigrants. We were active participants in this ministry and in 1981 we welcomed a Cambodian family of eight to live with us. The parents had witnessed the horrors of the Khmer Rouge regime between 1975 and 1979 and then lived for two years in a Thai refugee camp. We realized that their excitement for a new start was tempered by a fear of the uncertain future and the heavy weight of responsibility for six children: the oldest was 16 and the youngest was barely a month old. After moving to Massachusetts, our family endured many hardships including illness, prejudice, and arson but, thirty-five years later, the younger members of the original family are living throughout this country with their own children and grandchildren, businesses, and livelihoods.

When they first arrived, we helped our refugee family understand many aspects of American life, including banking, job hunting, and homework assignments, and we learned that friendly and kind teachers of English Language Learners (ELLs), which in those days we knew as students of English as a Second Language (ESL), provide a lifeline to those who enter the strange and unfamiliar world of the United States. Therefore, we continue to support ELL and ESL programs. We believe that being an ELL or ESL teacher is a tangible form of Christian hospitality; it can be as simple as showing the willingness to welcome others and help with life's questions. The Bible is clear about the importance of showing goodness to others and building bridges. "And you are to love those who are aliens, for you yourselves were aliens in Egypt" (Deut.10:19); "The king will reply, I tell you the truth, whatever you did for one of the least of these brothers of mine, you did for me" (Matt.25:40). The rewards of teaching are profound and humbling and learning about other cultures is endlessly enriching. English Language Learners/English As A Second Language programs not only benefit the learners, but volunteer teachers are often amazed at how much they learn from their students.

One of the most rewarding aspects of working with ELL/ESL is experiencing cross-cultural friendships. For example, in one class a student could not hold back her tears when describing how much she missed Brazil. She said that, despite the poverty she experienced there, she would always consider Brazil her home. She knows that the United States affords better opportunities for her children, yet she finds trying to keep her children from becoming materialistic Americans to be a daily challenge. The entire class, some from Korea, China, and Germany, could relate to her comments and their understanding was a comfort to her.

Volunteers serving ELL students are often the backbone of successful ESL programs based in public libraries and in churches and are the unsung heroes in many lives.

ESL IN PUBLIC LIBRARIES

The public library, known as the "people's university", is a natural place to host a volunteer ESL program. "Free to All" is inscribed on the outside of the Boston Public Library's Copley Square building. The inscription reminds Americans that the library is not an elite social club. In fact, there are no economic or educational barriers to prevent use of and access to the public library. All are welcome. Any volunteer ESL program, whether or not it meets in the public library, should be familiar with the local library's resources and introduce them to ESL participants.

Public libraries have a multitude of resources that benefit both ESL students and Adult Basic Education (ABE) students, including books in multiple formats, periodicals, DVDs, audiobooks, and music CDs, as well as literacy kits and other learning tools. Many libraries also lend items such as telescopes, iPads, and games. Programs, lectures, story times for children, and computers can benefit entire families. Many libraries offer passes and coupons for a reduced entrance fee at museums and local cultural institutions. Online resources available through many libraries enable patrons to continue learning at home at their convenience. Electronic resources such as Rocket Languages, Mango Languages, and Universal Class offer self-paced lessons. Peterson's Testing and Education Resource Center offers testing practice for the Test of English as a Foreign Language (TOEFL), Test of English for International Communication (TOEIC), and the U.S. Citizenship test. It is common for newcomers to be wary of new places and institutions, so the first step is to encourage ELL and ABE students to obtain their library cards. In most libraries, patrons will need to show identification and fill out a brief form. The entire process might take less than ten minutes, and the patron walks away with personal access to millions of items and resources. Since most online resources are barcode authenticated, the library card is necessary for off-site access. The Boston Public Library offers many literacy resources for ESL volunteers on the website at www.bpl.org. Also, the Boston Public Library allows all Massachusetts residents to obtain an e-card which gives them access to a large collection of e-books. Many countries do not offer the rich public library resources that are available in the United States, and students are often surprised and grateful to discover them.

TUTOR/LEARNER APPROACH

One model of library volunteer-based learning programs is to train volunteer tutors and then match each tutor with a learner for one-on-one tutoring. In a typical public library literacy program, there could be a variety of learners, some working on their General Educational Development (GED), others improving their English skills, while still others seeking help with job applications and resumes. In the 1990s, the Haverhill Public Library was the home of the Greater Haverhill Adult Learning Program which served ten communities in the Merrimack Valley of Massachusetts. Space to meet, computers with educational software, and a large collection of print resources were made available to tutors and learners. Once a volunteer tutor was matched with a learner, the pair would choose a mutually satisfactory schedule and meet weekly. The benefit of this approach is that the volunteer can understand the specific needs of the student and tailor the curriculum to those needs.

For example, a 25-year-old adult learner, who did not have a high school diploma, joined the free library-based literacy program, but he had little motivation to stay enrolled. Then his tutor discovered his secret dream of getting a driver's license. Though he knew how to operate a vehicle, he was never legally licensed. In order to achieve this goal, he and his tutor worked on an individualized plan. To begin, he had to accept the reality of the situation first and commit to solving the problem, then budget his resources to pay off all the accrued out-of-state fines and save up the money for the permit test. Finally, he needed to learn how to fill out all necessary paperwork for the Department of Motor Vehicles (DMV). All of this needed to be accomplished while studying the driver's manual in order to achieve an 80 per cent score on the permit test. The thought of taking the permit test on a computer created a lot of anxiety, so the tutor used the computers in the library to simulate the test he would take at the DMV testing stations. He started to gain confidence in learning to read material on the screen and answering the questions with the keyboard. This whole process took many months, but he stuck it out and eventually obtained his permit and license. Both the learner and volunteer were thrilled by this accomplishment.

CLASSROOM/CONVERSATION CIRCLE

At the Hamilton-Wenham Public Library in Hamilton, Massachusetts, group teaching is also very effective using either the traditional classroom approach or the conversation circle. It is important to get to know the students and communicate with them regularly, so students should fill out a brief intake form that includes their name, e-mail address, phone number, interests and hobbies, languages spoken, childcare needs, and desired outcomes for the class. Scheduling classes during school hours and evenings can alleviate some of the need for childcare, but a goal could also be for concurrent children's programming.

The conversation circle can be topical or literature-based and meets the needs of improving conversation skills. A literature-based group is very effective and librarians can help provide multiple copies of books in print and audio format for the class. The volunteer teacher should be prepared to offer historical background to the text, define vocabulary words, and lead a discussion. Some groups will relish having a chance to read aloud and work on pronunciation. Teachers should try to choose a book with literary merit regardless of the reading level. While advanced groups can tackle classics such as *O Pioneers* by Cather, books written for youth may be the most useful. Popular books at Hamilton-Wenham Public Library conversation circles have been *A Single Shard* by Park, *A Taste of Salt* by Temple, *Anne of Green Gables* by Montgomery, *Bread and Roses, Too* by Paterson and *Dragonwings* by Yep. Short stories are also good tools and The Cambridge University Press publishes a *Discovering Fiction* Series that includes short stories complete with lessons and homework assignments. It is important to encourage students to be immersed in the literature, keeping a dictionary handy but not necessarily looking up every unfamiliar word. This might be the first time a student has read a book in English and it is important that it be a pleasurable experience. In the public library setting, ELL students can easily graduate from a conversation circle to a regular monthly book club.

Dedicated and talented volunteers using public library space and resources make these programs successful. Library staff can facilitate by teaching groups basic library skills, assisting volunteers with administrative tasks and room set-up. Volunteers also need encouragement and praise for being so generous with their time and offering such an important service to others.

ESL AS A CHURCH MINISTRY

In Revere, Massachusetts, the First Congregational Church has always been community—minded, wanting to minister to the needs of the people in our city. We are a small church, but we magnify our impact by inspiring most of our members and attendees to get involved and use their God–given gifts. We have always had a heart for refugees and immigrants—strangers in our land. The Bible compels us to welcome the stranger. To address this one area, we are running an ESL program. It has been wildly successful in reaching out to our growing immigrant population.

WHAT IS OUR MISSION?

Our ESL ministry's purpose is to help the adult immigrants and refugees living in and near our city to learn the English language. It is a plain and simple goal but not an easy one to meet. We are not a school. We don't employ teachers. We don't have a vast pool of ESL-trained professionals involved. The best approach to learning English may depend upon why students want to learn it. Is it for a job, a career, or furthering their education? We have people in our city who need English for all of these reasons and more. We didn't think we could have an in-depth program that could meet the needs. We decided to start with a simple program. We use a basic ESL curriculum that is easy to teach. We use all volunteers who want to serve God and help people. We try to reach local residents who walk or take public transportation to our church. Most of our students have little experience learning English—they are self-taught, but they want to know more, and they are motivated!

In the fall of 2017, we began our eighth year of ESL in Revere. It is interesting to think back on how we started and the changes that have taken place. Our current program reaches out to the growing immigrant population in and around our city. Our church has been active in refugee and immigrant issues in the past. For a few years, a school teacher in our church was running a small evening ESL program in a public school in Revere. We also had an extensive refugee ministry that began with the Boat people of Vietnam in 1975 and continued sponsoring many refugees in a donated house in nearby Malden.

The current ESL program began in 2010 when an immigrant from Puerto Rico saw the need for English in his own family and friends and wanted to do something about it. He had benefited from ESL programs and asked why our church couldn't perhaps start one. In the fall of 2010, Fernando Gonzalez organized a simple start with two volunteer teachers. Our twenty adult students and neighbors were originally from Algeria, Colombia, Morocco, Palestine, Poland, and Syria. Their improved English skills would allow them to integrate better with and contribute to the local community.

The Ministry offered two 3-hour classes per week over a 12-week semester. The two classes were offered on Thursday morning and Thursday evening to best accommodate home and work obligations. The program was based on a professionally developed ESL program that included a student text, a workbook, and an audio CD with which students practiced lessons at home on their own time. The package also included reference materials for our volunteer teachers who gave their time and effort enthusiastically and maintained their supportive leadership throughout these early months.

Though both teachers had studied linguistics, the materials we used were written to allow any layperson to instruct a class. This included written and oral exercises and exams, as well as answer sheets. In addition to teachers we used conversation partners. These key personnel were used to offer an hour of weekly conversation and fellowship at a mutually convenient time and place with one or two students. This component gave our students a chance to exercise their training outside of a classroom setting, while offering other church volunteers an opportunity to demonstrate the thoughtful caring they had found through their Christian faith.

From its humble beginnings, our ministry grew slowly each year. At the same time, we noticed that the immigrant population in our city was growing. We were more and more convinced we were doing the right thing. Revere had previously welcomed immigrants particularly in the early twentieth century with large numbers of Italian migrants and Jewish migrants from Eastern Europe landing at our shores. Many of these people disembarked in Boston and eventually moved to the suburb of Revere, growing their family and becoming Americans. In the mid-twentieth century, Revere's population began to dwindle, and the stream of new migrants slowed to a crawl. Very few new immigrants or people of color were ending up in Revere.

Our own church began to lose members and become much smaller until a young pastor was hired as a last effort to revitalize the church. This effort was successful and many of the new members along with the pastor brought a fresh mix of ministry and faith to our church and city.

In 1975, as the Vietnam War was winding to a close for Vietnam with the fall of Saigon, millions of escaping refugees made their way to our country. Our church wanted to help and decided to sponsor a Vietnamese family. The family arrived in Revere, stayed with our young pastor, and was successfully integrated into American society. It certainly was not easy, but the church was excited. We wanted to do more. Other families sponsored refugees and they began coming from Vietnam and Cambodia. An enthusiastic former immigrant was led by God to donate a house he owned in nearby Malden to our new refugee ministry. We hired a part-time associate pastor to live in the house along with his family to fulfill their vision of starting a refugee ministry. Over the years, hundreds of refugees would pass through the doors of the house God provided.

As we saw the close of the twentieth century, our city was changing. With an older housing stock and lower rents, along with easy access to Boston, Revere was an inexpensive and convenient place to live. The working class, immigrants, and people of color were coming to the City of Revere to find a place to live.

With our active refugee ministry going on, a large influx of Southeast Asian refugees became residents of Revere. Soon the former Jewish neighborhood was transformed by new migrants and refugees. With former barriers broken, the inexpensive housing became an entry point for recent arrivals from Southeast Asia, Eastern Europe, Brazil, Morocco, and Central America. In the new century, we noticed this trend spreading across the whole city. As we walk through our city, we see a rich diversity of residents from all parts of the world. Once again, our city is welcoming immigrants. Our church members want to take part in helping new residents acclimate to our country and our city. We see that learning English is a key component of acclimation, but people are needed to provide that learning. God calls us to do it.

The necessities of migrants in our city are great. Sadly, government is often slow to adapt and respond. ESL programs in particular for our city are very limited. The Revere School System runs a program in the evenings, but it is small. Even the state programs do not have any real impact on Revere.

As we see the needs grow and grow, our church wants to become more involved and perform something meaningful and helpful and do God's work. By keeping our vision and ministry simple, we are able to use volunteers effectively to keep our costs low. By having our program during the day, we are able to reach out to women and mothers with young children who may be stuck at home with no easy options for learning English. We have the program in our church that is located in the middle of Revere and right on a bus route, so it is easy to get to. We have many servant opportunities for our eager helpers in teaching, substituting, assisting, administration, and childcare. We think our model can meet the needs in our City and perhaps be used as an example for other churches wanting to get involved in helping immigrants.

HOW WE DO IT

Our ESL program in Revere has evolved over the past eight years. We are five times larger and have reached the maximum we can accommodate within our current building at one time. We have many more volunteers and a childcare program to help parents with children who want to learn English. We have refined our intake process to better place new students in the proper class while expanding to five class levels. We try to increase our communication with our students to keep them motivated to complete the semester. With these changes, however, our vision is basically the same. So how exactly do we run our program?

As mentioned before, volunteers are an important key to our program. Working with volunteers is not always easy. Volunteers can be unreliable, self-centered, and hard to keep. But volunteers are wonderful! Volunteering is a noble pursuit and we need them, and they need to be appreciated, directed, and used wisely. Our director, who is also a volunteer, spends much time helping our volunteers, recruiting new volunteers, providing support services and encouraging them. We try to provide support for administrative tasks like registration, attendance management, classroom set up and materials and teaching aid acquisition, so our teachers can concentrate on teaching. Our goal is to have two teachers for each class along with one or two assistants. Many times, the two teachers may split the two-day schedule while others may take turns together teaching and assisting. Some teachers will split off some of their class who may need extra help to concentrate on a particular topic or lesson while the rest of the class proceeds.

Teachers love their students and do what they can to help them. Often a student may need extra help, encouragement to keep learning and studying, or just a friend to listen. Sometimes teachers may pray with a student if requested. Teachers often keep in touch with students through the mail or by text. For the teachers, it is about building a relationship of caring and encouragement with their students, that is what motivates them. That is why using volunteers can be so effective.

Often, there are not enough teachers for the ideal ratio of two per class, and we use assistants more actively, including former students. Assistants help with attendance, checking homework, or sometimes helping an individual student with a lesson. Many times, we start new volunteers as assistants, moving them among different classes, so they understand how we work. The assistants may not make as much of a commitment as a teacher does, and that works better for some volunteers. We can utilize their skills for a time and a season, and they may move on. Others stay devoted to one class for a long time. We can be flexible with assistants, accommodating their schedule and helping them to make a useful contribution to the program. In addition, teachers appreciate having one or two others in the classroom with them to be able to handle the workload.

Administrative duties for the program can be overwhelming. Without someone concentrating on the administrative tasks, the program can become ineffective. Teachers can arrive to their class knowing their space will be properly set up, that the students are aware of the schedule and have their books, and that if they need to take a day off a substitute will handle the class. Effective administration involves many outside-the-program hours sending out mailings, ordering materials, managing finances, promoting the ministry, prayer, and encouraging volunteers. Using volunteers has also allowed us to keep our costs low. Our current tuition is $60 per year, which includes a full set of student books.

A very important part of our program is child care. We may have up to 25 children ranging in age from newborn to over five-years-old in our playroom and nursery rooms for two hours. Our child care must not only be fun and safe for the kids—it must also instill a sense of trust in the parents. For many children this is the first time they have been separated from the parent for two hours in a strange place. They cry, they scream, and they don't want to come to the church. Parents have to know they trust us and will learn that their child will get used to being in the nursery or the play room and actually end up enjoying it.

Our child care volunteers play an important role in the ministry by playing and watching the children in their care but also building trust in parents. A worried parent will not be a good student in the classroom. In addition, a parent with a clinging child in the classroom will not be a good student. We do not let the students keep their children with them in class, so child care must work well.

We do have problems with child care. It is a difficult job, and it is hard to get regular volunteers. We encourage volunteers to come when they can even if it is once a month because we may need 6-8 child care workers on any given day. Sometimes we may not have enough coverage, which makes it extra difficult for those workers who are there. But for the volunteer who loves children and has God-given patience it is very rewarding. Cleaning playthings and toys takes time that our workers do not have. We must rely on our church and parents and the church nursery ministry to carry the load.

Security is another area that our program must address. We have all parents sign in and place a name tag on each child with their name and the parents name and class level. We have a checklist with the same information. Child care workers use this if they must get a parent from class and also at checkout time.

With the goal of focusing on teaching English in a clear and simple manner, we use materials from Cambridge University Press. Specifically, we use the Venture series. The series provides a student book for each student that is used in class and a workbook with a practice CD that is used at home and for homework and review. The series has a teacher's manual that includes the material in the manual side-by-side with in-class exercises, commentary on the material, and extra exercises, games, and activities that can be used during class time. Each lesson has a final test for teachers to use to measure the students' progress. The series also has other supplemental material and online resources for teachers. We have found that teachers can use the material for ESL without having to prepare a detailed lesson plan. We currently use the Basic series and Levels 1 -3. Each level includes 10 lessons and we spend a whole year (that is, two semesters) covering the 10 lessons. Also, the levels overlap, covering the topic at every level but from a different and more advanced perspective which reinforces student learning.

Teachers sometimes use their own materials or ideas. In our introductory class, we have tried to use the Ventures Basic series but have found that it is too advanced. Instead teachers focus on charts, pictures and sometimes children's books and tools to introduce letters, numbers, days, months, and other building blocks. It can be a challenge to help some students who may have had very little education even in their own language or whose native language uses a different character set than English. More advanced class level teachers use vocabulary and spelling with spelling tests and spelling bees to get students excited and motivated. Our most advanced class teacher has students write short stories about themselves and their experiences and write poetry as well as read.

A very useful tool available from Cambridge University Press is a simple placement test. We primarily use this short test to place new students in the proper level class. It matches our class levels based on the Venture series. It takes each prospective student 30-45 minutes to complete and is multiple choice. Sometimes, we also use the test once a student has completed a level of two semesters to determine if it is time to advance to the next level.

When we began the program, we had a single class for all students with the advantage being it was easier to accomplish and didn't require as many teachers. Through the past eight years we have evolved to fielding five class levels. The largest change was to add our introductory level that addresses students with no ability in English. The other classes, Basic, Level 1, Level 2 and Level 3, each match students to their ability according to the Ventures placement test or to the degree each student has advanced through the program from year to year. This has helped us to keep students of similar abilities together in a class level and not have some who are far too advanced or falling behind. Most students advance to the next level each year, but some may choose to stay with the advice of their teacher if they feel they really need to learn the material slowly before moving on. Some students need to grow in confidence. With Level 3 being our most advanced class, many students take the level for two or more years. The material used in this class varies the most from year to year, so students can stay in the program and continue to grow and practice their language skills and increase their confidence.

Our class size currently averages 16 to 22 students. We are somewhat limited by space. We have four classes in a large hall of the church that has very effective room dividers that run from floor to ceiling and keep sound from affecting the other classes in the room. We also have a class in our church library room and have another small classroom reserved for extra help space. More space and larger classrooms would make it easier to teach than in these crowded conditions. Our ideal class size might be 12-15 students, but we have found that class size tends to drop off during the course of a semester so many times we end up with this number near the end. It is important for a class size of 16-22 to have a larger staff as previously mentioned. Having assistants who can move around the classroom and help students when necessary is useful. In addition, teachers must closely monitor each student's progress. We encourage teachers to use the Venture series lesson tests to track progress through the year.

We take attendance in each classroom throughout the semester. At the end of each week, we collect the attendance sheets and send post cards to any student who has been absent for two or more classes. Sometimes we may also send a text message to the student's phone to remind them about class. These methods are somewhat effective in keeping students involved. Teachers also may communicate with students using text reminders or a phone call if a student has not been in class for two or three times. One teacher has started asking students to text him if they will be absent for a class. Using text can be simple and effective, but not all teachers may want to use their personal cell phone for ESL-related work. A drop-off in attendance and class size can be discouraging for teachers and students alike so we try to attack it and keep students motivated to come to class. For some semesters, we have a waiting list for classes that are full. When we have drop-outs, we try to backfill the student slots with those on the waiting list. Usually, by the third week in a 14-week semester, the class lists are stable.

An exciting part of our program is the end of the semester celebration. On the last day of class for each semester, we celebrate the students' achievements, have class presentations, and share a pot luck lunch together. Students receive a certificate for completion of the lessons during the semester. Students who have had perfect attendance are recognized with a special certificate. Each class puts on a demonstration of what they have learned. They may read stories they have written, act out skits, sing songs, play a game, or do a spelling bee, all to demonstrate together their new proficiency in English. Students are encouraged to bring a dish to share from their native country or their favorite local food. Many invite family members or friends to come and participate in the celebration. It is a wonderful culmination of the hard work and dedication that both students and teachers have accomplished during the semester. We also see it as another tool to keep us all motivated for learning and teaching English.

Our current program consists of two 14-week semesters each year, with twice weekly class sessions on Mondays and Wednesdays from 10 am to 12 noon. We start in September and break in December. We resume in January and end in May. We follow the local school system calendar, taking off school holidays, vacations, and snow days, which helps parents with children in school stay on the same schedule. We take a ten-minute break during each class session and serve coffee, tea, and snacks to the students. The students mingle in the open areas of the building, sharing their experiences with fellow students and chat with their teachers, helpers, and our church pastors. We have requests from some students to expand the program to Monday through Friday or longer class times. We have thought about expanding the class time, but teacher availability is the largest barrier. If we want to expand our program to have longer class times or open it up to more students on additional days or in the evening, we need more volunteer teachers and assistants. Right now, our current schedule is accommodating the immediate demand of the number of students who come to us seeking English classes. In the future, this may change. We are trying to follow God's plan for the ministry. We continue to see an increase in the number of non-English speakers and immigrants that move to Revere and surely demand for English classes will continue to grow.

We publicize the program primarily through word of mouth, newspaper articles, fliers, and post cards to our student database. Communication with other local English programs, our city government, the local school system, and state resources are other possibilities. We have done these things but find that word of mouth is the largest source of students. Being on a local referral list for immigrant services, however, is important so your program is recognized as a service point in your community where none other may exist.

RECENT YEARS—RESULTS

In the past eight years that our current program has been in place, we have seen growth in need and demand for English classes as the number of immigrants has grown. How successfully have we been meeting this demand in our service area? What changes will we need to make to accommodate students who want to learn English? How successful have we been in helping the many immigrants in our city? As we look at some of the results of our ministry program, we realize that we don't always know how well we are doing or how much we have accomplished. Part of the answer would be more measurement, follow-up surveys, and better statistics. As we grow, we may need to incorporate more of these tools into our work. Of course, we are meeting people's needs as we continue to grow and demand increases, however, it's also important to know how effective our methods, teaching, and materials are and have some basis for making that claim.

We have data on the numbers of students who enroll in our classes, how many complete our classes, our attendance, and how students have performed in class when the Ventures tests have been used consistently. The data needs to be better organized and tracked, so we can easily produce the statistics we need. Our growth is the easiest statistic to document, but we only need to look around us to prove that we are growing. We need to refine our data collection in future years, so we can produce statistics that will help us marshal the resources to continue the program. This exercise is something that can be ignored but should not be. It is very important for not-for-profit enterprises to have good statistics to start to prove their value and effectiveness. Statistics show results and results encourage supporters and enlist people to give money to the important job of teaching English to immigrants.

Many of the trends we see in our program and in Revere are experiential rather than those documented with statistics. As mentioned before, our growth seems to be driven more by the need and the number of immigrants coming to Revere rather than better publicity. In addition, over the past four years, more and more of our students are from Revere rather than surrounding communities. This may be due to a combination of more immigrants living in Revere and the availability of more local programs becoming available in surrounding cities. We are getting more students with no knowledge of English at all which would seem to indicate that there are more recent arrivals here now who need English. Certainly, the overwhelming numbers of students in our program are women. This is probably due to women in immigrant families staying home to take care of children or the number of men who are working and unable to come to day classes. We see this supported by the popularity of our child care program also. Our students typically come from upwards of 15 to 20 different countries in any given semester. The largest audience is from Central America with the next largest coming from Morocco. Spanish and Arabic are the two most common primary languages spoken. These trends match what we see going on in Revere that can be determined just walking the streets and noting the new storefronts and services that occupy our city.

What is the demand that is driving the growth of English language learners in our area and perhaps the entire country? We see it in our numbers, and we hear it from our students. Although our data is somewhat anecdotal, we can't ignore what they say. Immigrants need jobs to survive and they need English to get a job. Of course, there are many lower level service jobs that require little English out there. And certainly, on the job learning can be extended to learning English. Most of our students lament however that they can't learn English at work. They need to study English and learn it to advance or to get a decent paying job with which they can support their families.

Another reason our students say they want to learn English is to keep up with their kids. Many have expressed the frustration that they share with their children that as the kids grow they end up speaking two different languages and communication within the family becomes more difficult. Of course, this has been the plight of immigrants throughout our country's history. The difference today seems to be that immigrants want to do something about it either to keep their home bilingual with better communication or learn English so they can understand and help their children succeed in our growing knowledge economy.

Additional motivation for learning English is citizenship. If immigrants are eligible to apply for citizenship, they must learn English. Certainly no one knows what the immediate future hold for immigrants in our country. Immigrants with documentation don't know if the right to become a citizen may be taken away, and they don't want to risk that. Undocumented immigrants don't know if some day amnesty may be negotiated and certainly want to know English to participate.

As the ministry in our church has progressed, so has the support and participation of our church members. Most of our volunteer teachers and assistants are from our church, which is an increase in congregational participation over the past few years. Our child care workers are all members. We regularly talk about the ministry on Sunday mornings and ask for help and prayer. Our two pastors visit our classes on both days to talk briefly with students and staff. In general, we have more volunteers working on the program than ever before. Word has spread, and it's an exciting place to be for at least 22 volunteers. In addition to church members, we have volunteers from our community, former students, and volunteers from distant suburbs involved. The program has become widely known and attracts those who want to help immigrants and refugees but may not get that opportunity in their own town or church. These are all fantastic developments for our ministry, enabling us to do a better job helping people learn English while we inspire volunteers and help them to grow.

REAL LIFE STORIES

As I, Michael, sat talking to potential students, I had to tell them we were full. With classes all at their maximum all we could do was keep a waiting list. The next woman came with a young child; she had been a student a few years previously but wasn't able to continue. She inquired about the current classes. I explained again that the program was full, and she could only sign up for the waiting list. She filled in the form and as I gave her a receipt she began to cry. She needed to study English; she was depressed at home, did I understand, could I help her? I tried to calm her down and explained I would do my best to fit her in somehow. Later, as I looked at our class attendance to see where we might have an opening I thought about how desperate she sounded and felt very sad myself. Even the small amount of language study we offered four hours per week was often a lifeline to the future for our students. I hadn't really thought of it that way. I was able to find a slot in the class she needed and asked the teacher if she could take one more. I notified her by text the next day and received back a "thank you." When she arrived the following week, she had a smile on her face and was ready to learn English once again. She joined the other students working diligently to climb that next step up the ladder of American life.

All of our teachers are dedicated to helping students and volunteer their time freely. One teacher who demonstrates that dedication is Jane. She travels to Revere twice per week by train, subway, and bus, a trip that often takes two hours each way. She is 70 years old and shows no sign of stopping. She has volunteered at schools closer to her home but chooses to spend most of her efforts at our school. She loves the students and is inspiring to the advanced students in our Level 3 class. Many students return again to take the class to be able to spend time learning from Jane. She grew up as a missionary child and learned the importance of learning and teaching languages. We are certainly blest to have her on our staff.

Some of our students start at the beginning and faithfully advance through the program. From Basic to Level 3 takes four years of study. One such student is Mary. She and her husband are from Honduras and came to the United States several years ago. They both have worked very hard and began raising a family, bought a house, and settled in Revere. They realized, however, that without English they would be stuck with low paying jobs and not able to communicate with their own children. One day they stumbled upon our program with a flier that a friend gave them. They came, and both signed up for Basic English. Mary stayed home with her children while her husband worked nights at a cleaning job. Our classes on weekday mornings were perfect for both of them. They worked hard that first year and continued to move through each level. When they reached Level 3, you could see the difference in language skills from when they began. Mary was much more confident and was very proud of her hard work during our end of the year celebration. I asked her about her plans, did she want to take the class again or would she move on to another program? She smiled and asked if she could volunteer and help others learn English. The program had been so helpful to her she wanted to share it. She was able to communicate with her growing children who were now proficient in English. However, she wanted to be useful and put her new skills to the test. That next year, she began helping in our Level 1 class but, when we started our new Introduction to English class, we really needed her. Mary has found her niche helping us translate for Spanish speakers, especially those who know no English at all. This has been a terrific need met and has enabled our Introductory class to be successful.

Last year, a student from El Salvador confided to her teacher that she was about to be thrown out of her cousin's home where she, her husband, and her son were living. There were family problems. Johanna continued her story and asked the teacher to pray for her son who was the reason they were in the United States. He suffered from a form of leukemia and was here for treatment that he could only receive in this country. They had sacrificed so much to be here and couldn't afford to be homeless. The teacher quickly notified others, and we began to pray for her son and a solution to her immediate problem. One of our pastors got involved and met Johanna's husband to see how we might help. He invited the couple and their son to come to church on Sunday. The family did come and met many concerned people who promised to pray too. Thanks to the pastor's intervention, the family problems eventually were worked out and they were able to stay in their home. Their son kept up treatment and his condition improved. The family comes to church because they are thankful for the concern of their new-found friends. Johanna is back again to our ESL program to continue her study of English.

WHERE DO WE GO FROM HERE WITH OUR LIMITS OF SPACE, FACILITY ITEMS, VOLUNTEERS, AND TIME?

This year, as we have seemed to have reached our limits of what we can easily do, we are thinking about the future and looking to God to direct us. What can we do to help all the people who need to learn English in our city?

There seems to be no limit to the need right now but, of course, that could change in the future. We are limited by space, our volunteers, availability, and even things like the number of chairs and tables we have available. Of course, we also know that our God is a boundless God who can provide whatever we need to be able to do His work. So, we will continue to seek His will on our future direction to deal with all our Revere immigrants and their need for English.

We know and have seen that our immigrant friends have many more needs besides learning English. We have been challenged by our students' need of affordable housing, better jobs, reliable childcare, help with their children's schools, immigration issues, legal matters, adequate healthcare, and spiritual needs. Often these needs come up in class or in discussions students may have with their teachers. We may be able to address a need here or there, but we too are overwhelmed by the issues they face. These issues can be overcome; some of them are faced by all residents of our city. We also are seeking what—if anything else—we can do to help our immigrant friends.

Our church has been planning to rehabilitate some unused space we have in our church office building. This space when developed would offer more classroom and general meeting space for our programs. Our current crowded classes could at least spread out for a less cramped learning experience. One of our teachers has started a fund-raising campaign to help our program. We plan on using these funds to purchase additional tables and chairs to accommodate our students better. And, as previously mentioned, we are excited about the support we are receiving and the number of volunteers who are participating in our program. We plan on continuing to expand our staff, especially former students and assistants to provide more one-on-one assistance and follow-up with students who could benefit from the help. We will continue to seek what God would have us do and rely on His love through us for the strangers in our land.

In conclusion, ESL is a program that offers growth, friendship and encouragement to both teachers and students. ESL changes lives. We deeply appreciate all of our co-laborers and hope that many more will be inspired to join this effort.

Part Two:

Strategies of Christian Teachers
in a Christian Setting

Chapter Six

Teaching Migrant Children Prepared Me to Teach Theology to At-Risk ELL

JEANNE DEFAZIO

INTRODUCTION

OVER THE PAST NINE years as an Athanasian Scholar (teaching associate) working in Dr. William Spencer's Systematic and Contemporary Theology courses, I adapted teaching techniques to the learning needs of culturally diverse English Learning students. I am participating in this dialogue to make these techniques available for those who teach English Language Learners and because I believe that any English Language Learner (ELL) can master Systematic and Contemporary Theology at Gordon-Conwell Theological Seminary (GCTS) given the proper teaching strategies.

PRAYER AS A SPIRITUAL STRATEGY TO ENCOURAGE ENGLISH LANGUAGE LEARNERS

"Teachers can foster oneness of knowledge by making connections across subjects and bringing these to students' notice, showing how faith plays a role in history, science, or literature."[1]

---

1. "What is Learning?," lines 28–29.

At the beginning of each class, Dr. Spencer calls the Athanasian scholars to address the students. Each time, I pray Daniel 1:17[2] over the entire class, asking God to give each aspiring theologian the unusual aptitude for learning given to Daniel and his friends: Hananiah (Shadrach), Mishael (Meshach), and Azariah (Abednego) in the court of the Babylonian king. Beyond development of teaching strategies, I ask the Lord to open the mind of each student supernaturally.

Jozy Pollock spent years as a chaplain in the Los Angeles Penal System. In a recent interview, she mentioned an inmate's remarkable supernatural aptitude for learning: "A man in his fifties came into my office while I was a chaplain at the Los Angeles Jail. He told me he had never learned to read. He had been given a Bible and miraculously he was able to read it. He was not able to read a newspaper or a magazine or anything else other than the Bible."[3]

James 1:5 reminds us that God gives wisdom, knowledge, and skill.[4] I remind my students of Scripture's promises that God will foster the believer's learning.

As an Athanasian scholar, I realize my purpose is to make certain that English Language Learners grasp the basic tenets of orthodox Christian theology and meet the requirements of the class assignments and the work cover sheets. In this chapter, I will identify two very important strategies to accomplish this goal: eye contact in communication and reducing anxiety for English learners.

---

2. Daniel 1:17: "*God gave them knowledge, aptitude for learning, and wisdom. Daniel also could understand all kinds of visions and dreams.*" (ISV)

3. Jozy Pollock interview by email, May 4, 2017. Hear more of what Jozy has to say in the biographic" On Faith Alone" by Aimee Kozell available on YouTube: https://www.youtube.com/watch?v=auNvGVfes5U&t=7s. Jozy Pollock and Mel Novak's *review* of Jesus and Magic *is published in the Africanus Journal Volume 9, Number 1, April 2017:* http://www.gordonconwell.edu/resources/documents/AfricanusJournal91e.pdf.   *Mel Novak's teaching airs on Omega Man Radio:* "You're a candidate for a Miracle"—Mel Novak—Omega Man *https://www.youtube.com/watch?v=Dn5XG3LOvoE.*

4 James 1:5: "If any of you lacks wisdom, you should ask God, who gives generously to all without finding fault, and it will be given to you" (NIV). "Alexander Maclaren; Lacks (3007) (leipo) (repeated from Jas 1:4-note) means falling short, being destitute or being in need. It pictures one not possessing something which is necessary. James does not want his readers to be deficient in anything that reflects Christian maturity. Wisdom (4678) (sophia) is the ability to judge correctly and to follow the best course of action, based on knowledge and understanding." James 1:5-6 Commentary, http://www.preceptaustin.org/james_15–6.

FACE TIME WITH ENGLISH LANGUAGE LEARNERS

Face time with English Language Learners is a key strategy. I find that North and South American students are often more at ease in making eye contact with teachers while Asian students are inclined, due to specific politeness rules, to wait until the teacher makes eye contact to respond. Kinesic learning[5] is essential to the development of reading, writing, and speaking skills. English Language Learners adapt to the nonverbal cues the teacher gives to determine the meaning of the words they are learning. To minimize their anxiety (which can have a damaging effect on comprehension of subject matter and classroom performance), I dialogue verbally and kinesically with a synchronized rhythm. [6]

Masahiro Kawasaki, Yohei Yamada, Yosuke Ushiku, Eri Miyauchi, and Yoko Yamaguchi, in the *Scientific Reports* article, entitled *Inter-brain synchronization during coordination of speech rhythm in human-to-human social interaction* explain synchronized rhythm:

> Individual human behavioral rhythms in nature are independent but can be spontaneously synchronized and entrained to become a shared rhythm through interactions with others (i.e., social interactions) by both verbal and nonverbal communication. We experience daily synchronizations with others, such as with hand clapping or foot tapping and incidental coordination of speech frequencies in conversations. This unconscious, shared rhythm brings individuals close to each other, generates empathy, and coordinates performance.[7]

While teaching, I often begin a sentence and prompt the English learner to repeat and/or eventually complete it. While it appears that I am using a lot of gestures while I speak, such actions are intentional because gestures with words supplement a great deal in communication.

I developed this technique watching Dr. Spencer, who gestures effectively and emphatically while lecturing. If you click the linked footnote, you will understand what I am talking about.[8] Many gestures are

---

5. "Kinesics is the study of the way in which certain body movements and gestures serve as a form of non-verbal communication." Wikipedia, "Kinesics."

6. Clair and Giles, *The Social and Psychological Context of Language*, 108.

7. Kawasaki, Yamada, Ushiku, Miyauchi, and Yamaguchi, "Inter-brain synchronization during coordination of speech rhythm in human-to-human social interaction," lines 19–27.

8. DeFazio, *Creative Ways to Build Christian Community Non GCTS Promotional*

idiosyncratic. For example, the American television commentator Walter Cronkite blinked when he placed extra emphasis on words during a broadcast. The baby boomer generation will never forget Cronkite's blink as CBS interrupted *As The World Turns* on November 22, 1963 to announce the assassination of JFK.[9]

It is helpful if, as a teacher, I watch for words and gestures of English Language Learners that indicate they are experiencing cognitive difficulty and anxiety during a lesson. They may gaze away from the teacher or may continue to make eye contact moving eyes from right to left while processing unfamiliar subject matter. When this happens, I repeat the lesson until a student's body language indicates understanding. Speaking slowly and repeating a new concept using new vocabulary allows English learners to mimic the teacher. Repeating a concept and new vocabulary several times allows students to repeat new information until they're comfortable with the knowledge. This becomes less tedious if I vary the gestures associated with the new vocabulary. After going over a lesson in conversation, I ask each student to follow up with a written outline to demonstrate ownership of the basic doctrines of orthodox Christianity. If the first draft does not indicate comprehension of a subject, I meet face to face again with the student repeating vocabulary and key concepts. I keep account of the students' English reading, writing, and speaking progress. If there is a concept a student is not mastering, I ask him/her to reread a definition from a required text aloud, then to close the book, and to explain the concept in his/her own words. Then I ask the students to integrate the concept in the written requirements of the course. I repeat this process until the students can make eye contact using the vocabulary in conversation and describe the theological concepts in written course requirements. When the students stumble, I remind them that I could not read, write, or speak about Christian doctrines in their native languages, and I applaud their efforts to go the extra mile to express what they know in English.

Adult English Language Learners need coping skills to reduce anxiety. The inability to use a reasonable number of words can provoke anxiety. I repeat vocabulary to create a low stress learning environment. According to Radcliffe and McKoon's *Modeling the Effects of Repetition and Word*

Video; 2014 09 27 https://youtu.be/DK6F_TUH8Ug.

9. CBS Newsflash from Nov. 22nd 1963 Re: The JFK Assassination, https://youtu.be/c7fCpdvcl7k.

Frequency, modelling and repetition are key to English learning.[10] In an interview, Michelle DeFazio, MLIS, detailed a parallel example, tutoring a conversationally fluent dyslexic by repeating words while tracing the words simultaneously. She explained that sometimes dyslexic learners aren't predominately visual or audio but kinesthetic learners as well and rely more heavily on a combination of seeing, hearing, and tracing words to learn. This combination of strategies developed her student's literacy.[11] I adapt this high sensory strategy for English Language Learners when they are challenged to identify a theological concept in their papers requiring the use of unfamiliar sight words (words that are exceptions to grammatical rules). I trace the words on paper several times while repeating the words for emphasis.

REDUCING ANXIETY

"Laughter is the closest thing to the grace of God." Karl Barth[12]

My students and I have fun and laugh a lot. This is not exactly a teaching strategy, but, if I can get the student to see the humorous side of a situation, that helps them tremendously. If I see the student's attention waver, I usually add a funny comment to allow them to feel more at ease with the subject matter. I laugh at their jokes, which is part of honoring the unique quality of their thinking.

In the classroom, laughter erupts from relief over the edits of a draft, surprise at how well the work is progressing, and joy most of all when a student ends the course with success. Church Planter and Former Secretary of Training and Personnel Development of the Presbyterian Church of East Africa Reverend Dr. Lawrence PK Mbagara, Pastor of Gateway Church of Boston observes the members of his congregation feel uplifted in a community of laughter and love that is modeling the joy of the Lord as their strength (Neh. 8:10). I have included a link to Gateway' worship service to show that edifying joy in action. The Lord loves to see joy and hear praise inside the classroom and the sanctuary.[13]

10. Radcliffe and McKoon, "Modeling the Effects of Repetition and Word Frequency."

11. DeFazio, MLIS, interview by email and phone, May 15, 2017.

12. Wikiquote, "Karl Barth," line 23.

13. Reverend Dr. Lawrence PK Mbagara, Pastor of Gateway Church of Boston, interview in person May 25, 2017. Click this link to view Gateway Presbyterian Church of Boston worship service: https://youtu.be/csjVbnzHkMc.

To create a low stress learning environment a happy mistake zone is essential. A positive attitude toward making mistakes is important. If students overcome fear of grammatical error, they focus on content. If a student can express anxiety, that helps them. English Language Learners are often anxious about expressing themselves due to poor basic writing mechanics, weakness of grammar, lack of vocabulary, and spelling skills. If they feel free to admit to these challenges, that clears the air. I encourage students by explaining that the flow of ideas is more important than grammatical correctness. It is important for the teacher to validate the student's effort on the first draft. Usually, the students' confidence is not affected by errors in written work if I explain how to reorganize the work and emphasize how the mistakes in the first draft empower their learning process. If a student is lost in translation but comprehends the subject matter, it is apparent on the first draft. After rewriting and submitting a second draft, the student realizes how much knowledge he/she has gained through the process and that builds confidence.

I go over assignments and course cover sheet requirements repeatedly and specifically with each student, so they understand where their work needs adjustment. Improving the English Language Learners' writing skills is a creative process which involves drafting and editing and incorporating teacher's feedback. In this long process, the students gain vocabulary and confidence identifying Christian doctrine in English. The strategies indicated: eye contact, understanding the social and psychological context of language (kinesics), and a positive attitude toward making mistakes depends on constructive feedback from the teacher.

Praising the student's efforts is essential. Award-winning, multi-talented vocalist and songwriter Sheri Pedigo recently taught a vocal class in Culver City Community College. I am including the link to Sheri's course in this chapter to identify the way that encouragement from a mentor and teacher can improve the performance of the student. [14]

14. Sheri Teaching a Vocal Class in Culver City Community College Part 1, https://www.youtube.com/watch?v=U-EvrdioaVg. Sheri's review of Michele Pillar's autobiography *Untangled*, is *published in the Africanus Journal Volume 9, Number 1, April. 2017*, http://www.gordonconwell.edu/resources/documents/AfricanusJournal91e.pdf.

INSTRUCTIONAL METHODOLOGY

How did I learn to teach so intentionally? My educational background is a factor. I received a BA in History from the University of California at Davis, an MAR in Theology from Gordon-Conwell Seminary, and completed the Cal State Teach English Language Learners program. I hold a California Pre-K through 12 Multiple Subject Credential and an Adult History Certificate.

My mother has been a role model in my life. I am including details of her life to identify the extent of her positive influence. If my mother had not worked in the fields as a child laborer with her mother, brother, and sisters during the Depression and then served to make a difference in the lives of English Language Learners in a Nutrition Advocate Program for Yolo County's migrant workers children,[15] attended Catholic schools and excelled as an English Language Learner, and then, as an adult, tutored English Language Learners voluntarily in the Davis Joint Unified School District,[16] I would never have taught migrant workers' children in the seasonal workers' camp in North Davis, California. I would never have taught Hispanic students in the barrios in San Diego, California, or English Language Learners at the Center for Urban Ministerial Education at Gordon-Conwell Theological Seminary Boston Campus.

If my mother did not stand up for the rights of the oppressed as a Gospel Justice Catholic activist at St. James Catholic Church[17] in Davis, California, continuing to make a difference in the lives of marginalized members of her community throughout her life, at eighty protesting the lack of benefits for University of California at Davis food servers and having her photo appearing in the front page of *The Davis Enterprise*[18] with a rosary in her hand standing up for the rights of the underprivileged,[19] there would be no photos of me on Sproul Plaza during the Free Speech Movement, as a

---

15. Shipley Walters, in her book, *From Pantry to Food Bank: The First Forty Years: A History of the Food Bank,* details Inez' input in the North Davis camp summer food program: "During the last two months of August each summer, Economic Opportunity Program served meals in the Migrant Laborers camp in North Davis. Inez DeFazio provided training to site staff and their supervisors and communicated tirelessly with school administrators, county organizers, and government agencies, to keep the program running smoothly." Walters, *From Pantry to Food Bank,* 17.

16. Davis Joint Unified School District: Home Page *www.djusd.k12.ca.us/.*

17 Gospel Justice Ministry, St. James Catholic Church, *https://www.stjamesdavis.org/.*

18. The Davis Enterprise, *www.davisenterprise.com.*

19. Inez DeFazio, interview in person, April 30, 2017.

member of Berkeley Street Theatre,[20] performing in Gospel-based theater. If it weren't for my mother's unshakable faith in Jesus as a Roman Catholic Christian, I would never have considered ministry. If it were not for my mother's concern for the marginalized, I would not have done missionary work among the untouchables with Mother Teresa and the Sisters of Charity. If my mother had not been an example as a community organizer in the Economic Opportunity Program of Yolo County and a co-founder of the Yolo County Food Bank,[21] I would not have organized Christian community meals for the homeless in New York City while working for Michael P. Grace II.

PRIOR EXPERIENCE TEACHING
ENGLISH LANGUAGE LEARNERS

Before teaching theology learners at CUME, I had three brief but notable experiences teaching English language learners. I would like to comment on these, as they each fed into one another and into my current work with Dr. Spencer's class at Gordon Conwell's Boston/CUME.

North Davis Camp

As I noted, as a college student, I taught migrant workers' children one summer in the late 1960s. The laborers at the camp were my age and all the teenage women had young children. Each morning, the mothers handed me their preschool children and worked eight hours in triple digit sun temperatures, bent over the debilitating short handled hoe,[22] harvesting crops while the students and I sat under fans in the makeshift classroom.

At that time, I had no formal knowledge of California Public School System Teaching Standards. The teaching strategies I used in that classroom

---

20. See DeFazio, *Berkeley Street Theatre.*

21. Yolo County Food Bank, http://www.yolofoodbank.org/.

22. "The human damage caused by long-term use of short-handled hoes, which required the user to bend over from the waist to reach the ground, and caused permanent, crippling lower back pain to farm workers, resulted, after struggle led by César Chávez with political help from Governor Jerry Brown in the California Supreme Court, in declaring the short-handled hoe to be an unsafe hand tool that was banned under California law in 1975." Wikipedia, "Hoe tool," lines 47–48.

are ones that I learned to identify years later while completing my Teaching Credential program at Cal State Teach.

Nursery rhymes and children songs with finger play were very popular with the students. My long-time colleague, Jane Porter, a librarian, has implemented many programs for English language learners. In her interview with me, which she entitled *Storytimes in 13 Languages: How One Library Responded to Unite a Multicultural Community*, she notes and models the power of singing and finger play as a preparation to teach English Language Learners reading. I include Jane's entire interview to give the reader creative ways to teach ELLs:

"Twinkle, twinkle, little star. . .the melody begins, but this time, the words are in Chinese. A group of preschool children sing along as their mothers coach them and remind them of the corresponding finger plays. Later, we hear the same melody, but this time, the words are in French. The next day, another group is being led by an Arabic speaker, or Japanese, or Hebrew, or Italian, Hindi, Portuguese, or Korean. One could stop in for a story time in up to 13 different languages to reflect this multicultural library community.

Even more interesting are some of the language overlaps. We observe a Hebrew mom and her children enjoying the Arabic story time and the Korean mom bringing her children to the Japanese story time. Later, when another parent arrives at the library and hears about the story times in various languages, he asks, "How come no Portuguese?" and staff would reply, "We would love that. Could you teach it?" Shortly after, Portuguese story time is added to the calendar.

This program began with a group of moms and their young preschoolers meeting in the library for English story time and for socializing after. When various groups speaking in multi-languages revealed themselves, staff would ask, "Would one of you like to lead a story time in your native language?" Eventually, the languages multiplied and one day, a group of Spanish moms were meeting in the nearby park. Staff invited them into the library with, "By the way, would you like to have a regular story time in Spanish?"

Word must have gotten around and another day a group of mostly Chinese moms appeared in the story time circle and began an impromptu story time. Of course, we asked them if they would like to make it a regular event.

The leaders of these groups, mostly stay-at-home moms with small children, or sometimes volunteers, organized themselves according to their own available time, and some would do a craft while others would add movement. When we had the opportunity, we would add books to the collections in the various languages.

The story times became happy times for the moms and families and a way for the community to connect. It was not unusual for the families to spend time after the story times socializing with the other moms.

The library provides the slot on the calendar and the location, and the books when possible. If we could arrange a leader, we did. Sometimes staff that spoke Russian or other languages would lead, or sometimes the groups would find a leader. Sometimes staff would reach out and find a leader. Some story times had more music and songs than others and some only had a reader. Often, the groups grew because the participants were sharing with others that they knew. Eventually, 13 different groups were meeting with story times in 13 different languages.

The children benefitted because the story times helped prepare the preschoolers for when they would start school. Children were learning how to attend and how to hold a book, do finger plays, and perform other skills important for early language development and as preparation for reading. The library increased its visibility in the community. The families learned about the other activities available at the library and attended other scheduled events. Sometimes, recordings were made of the popular English story times, as the families were leaving to return to their home country, and the children wanted a reminder of Mr. Wiggle and Mr. Waggle, a popular story time, incorporating finger plays instead of a book.

Encouraging the library community to engage in their own native languages resulted in programming enrichment that was fun, supported literacy and early learning, and expanded community connections."[23]

My experience in the North Davis Camps with the children was similar to Jane's. Singing in Spanish with English translation is a wonderful way to teach Hispanic English learners. [24]

23. Jane Porter, MLIS, interview by email, May 14, 2017.

24. Martha Reyes, international vocalist, psychologist and founder of Hosanna Foundation, provides a bilingual (Spanish/English) website, wherein her songs combine English and Spanish. This is a valuable tool to encourage Hispanic English Language Learners. Martha Reyes website: http://www.marthareyes.com/. Martha Reyes' review of *Integrative Approaches to Psychology and Christianity* is published *in the Africanus Journal Volume 9, Number 1, April 2017:* http://www.gordonconwell.edu/resources/documents/ AfricanusJournal91e.pdf. *Click this link to hear Martha* Reyes's Musica Catolica Cristiana www.Catolicatv.com. https://www.youtube.com/watch?v=3ottIfSHvlg.

My students were happy to teach me the Spanish words of English nursery rhymes and songs and I was delighted that they learned so much English in the role reversal.[25] It benefited the children to see me go through the learning process. Experts in the field of English as a Second Language explain that certain linguistic and cognitive strategies reduce the English Language learners' anxiety.[26] As long as I let the children teach me Spanish, they had no anxiety as English learners. They only laughed at my pronunciation of Spanish occasionally. It broke the ice, so when they mispronounced English, there was no performance anxiety issue. Apart from a few dental and medical problems for which the Yolo County Health and Human Services[27] provided available clinics, these children were healthy, happy, avid learners.

The strategy of role reversal helped the students develop cognitive abilities which improved their English fluency. Thought processing English nursery rhymes and songs in Spanish was a bridge that carried the students into English literacy. Experts agree that achievement is generally higher in Hispanic English Language Learners who are taught in bilingual programs. This could be described as a modified bilingual program[28] because other bi-lingual staff pitched in and translated what I could not to the students. Students' confidence rose as their English vocabulary increased. Role reversal encouraged emotional growth as well as intellectual development and kept the mood in the classroom light. It allowed me to see how the students comprehended English. If there were words the students did not understand, it became apparent as they taught, and I intervened and explained what each did not fully grasp. A modified communicative approach[29] focuses on the practical end of learning. Gradually, the students expressed what was most important to them in simple English short phrases.[30] They

25. "Role Reversal—Teacher role-plays as the student, asking questions about the content. The students are collectively the teacher, and must answer the questions. Works well as test review/prep." "Interactive Techniques," 13. Adapted from Angelo and Cross, *Classroom Assessment Techniques.* Morrison-Shetlar and Marwitz, *Teaching Creatively.* McGlynn, *Successful Beginnings for College Teaching.* Silberman, *Active Learning: 101 Strategies to Teach Any Subject.* Gundy, *101 Activities for Teaching Creativity and Problem Solving.* Watkins, *75 e-Learning Activities: Making Online Learning.*

26. Qashoa, *English Writing Anxiety.* 1.

27. Yolo County Health and Human Services, http://www.yolocounty.org/health-human-services.

28. Strohman, *Methods for Teaching Hispanic English Language Learners,* 8.

29. Ibid.

30. Learning language successfully comes through having to communicate real meaning. Ibid, 9.

learned to use their words in English to ask for food, request permission to use the bathroom, to explain if they were feeling ill or needed a nap or an exercise break.

It was apparent to me that, because I was teaching younger students who were among peers, that the students learned more English than I did Spanish, but I did learn a few conversational Mexican phrases. I look back on this as my introduction to teaching English Language Learners with gladness at their progress and wondering where these students ended up after these forty plus years. I am certain that our cultural exchange was mutually beneficial.

SUBURBAN AFRICAN-AMERICAN HIGH SCHOOL

My next teaching experience was at a large suburban high school in Maryland. This was a pre-Columbine[31] primarily African-American community with highly publicized gun and knife fights, where drugs on campus were common. This high school, in 1997, boasted an affluent middle-class community. The student body drove late model cars and ordered pizza in for lunch. The English reading levels of some of many of the students was below grade level and the adolescents may have known how to speak English, but as a cultural distinction chose to use a ghetto talk[32] rather than speak English according to instruction. This became an issue with many of the African-American teachers who wanted the students to speak Standard English to generate success in the professional world. There were a few ways that I was able to break through with these students. I found slang culturally fascinating and asked the students to translate it for me. As a communicative strategy, I created word exercises where the students substituted slang for Standard English pronunciation. The students thought this was fun. It became apparent to me that the students had strong cultural ties to the slang they used. In translation the students were able to tell me about themselves in a transformational way. One day, a student who seemed to be progressing with this communicative approach to English learning told

31. The Columbine High School Massacre was a school shooting among Anglo-Americans that occurred on April 20, 1999, at Columbine High School, an unincorporated area of Jefferson County in the State of Colorado. Wikipedia, "Columbine High School Massacre."

32. "Ghetto talk is the usage of informal words and slang in sentences." http://www.urbandictionary.com/define.php?term=Ghetto%20Talk.

me after class that he made a wrong move in a drug connection that day and he was afraid he was going to die. I had no trouble believing this young man was telling me the truth. There was no text book strategy for conflict resolution that came immediately to my mind. So, I called in a veteran inner city African-American teacher. She was a Christian and the faculty was very tolerant of her praying with students in the classroom despite the fact that this was a Maryland public school.

After the teacher prayed for the student during an art class he drew a picture. In it there was a face of a young African-American boy who had a tear falling from one eye. He explained to me that, as an initiation into the gangs, the boy in the picture killed someone and that is why he had a tear drawn under his eye. He broke through in art and expressed his feeling he was not able to express verbally. This was a visual strategy to English learning.[33] Charlene Eber, in her review of *The Energy of Forgiveness*, explains that many people experience deep forgiveness without ever using the language of forgiveness.[34] That is what I believe happened for this young man after prayer. His artwork was a restorative path to healing his wounds.

The African American teacher's prayer and that art class were "safe spaces" for this young man whose life was gripped by violence. April Shenandoah in her review of *Just Peace: Ecumenical, Intercultural and Interdisciplinary Perspectives* cites the courage of those who build a peaceful community by creating safe spaces for children, allowing them to express their sorrows and joys.[35] I detailed this teaching experience as I believe that this teacher's prayer and the student's drawing model "peace education."

I mention this incident to underscore the need for teachers to pray for students. As I mentioned in my book, *Creative Ways to Build Christian Community*, Yvonnette O'Neal, who taught inner city students at the famous "Fishing School" in South East DC,[36] is combatting the culture of violence by implementing Bible Clubs in the public-school system. As a mentor, teacher and intercessor, she skillfully integrates prayer and Bible study into the lives of inner city children: Yvonnette is quick to remind young inner-city men and women of God's promise in 1 John 5:14: "We

33. Garcia, "Usage of Multi-Media Visual Aids in the English Language Classroom," 2.

34. Eber, Review of *The Energy of Forgiveness*, 47.

35. Shenandoah, Review of *Just Peace*, 59.

36. DeFazio and Lathrop, *Creative Ways*, 24.

have confidence in approaching God, if we ask anything according to His will, He hears and answers our prayers."[37]

CAL STATE TEACH PROGRAM STUDENT TEACHING

Much of what keeps the culture of violence alive is reacting to ongoing prejudice. While volunteering on a United States government office's comment line, I took a call from an outraged woman from the Midwest who said indignantly that Hispanics we're moving into her community. Proper comment line procedure is to state, "I have to take another call now, please write to your senator or congressman." I hung up and thought about my mom who always believed that within her Hispanic DNA was the ability to make a difference. I loved the fact that she loved being Hispanic. I didn't understand why she was so adamant about her love of the Hispanic culture until that day when the distraught woman yelled on the phone at me. She was complaining to me because she was certain I would not be working on that comment line and be Hispanic. I realized that my mother's staunch support of all things Hispanic was born of years experiencing cultural prejudice she never mentioned.

Cultural prejudice is something that each of us with predominately minority backgrounds at one point or another has experienced.[38] Such incidents of cultural prejudice drove me to leave Washington D.C., enroll in an English learner's teaching credential program at Cal State Teach,[39] and begin student teaching in San Diego, California. In the barrio, I taught classes with only Hispanic students. The students knew my Spanish was limited, though that was half of my ethnic background but gave me the opportunity to teach them English. When I did not understand what my

37. Yvonnette O'Neal interview by phone and email, May 14, 2017. Click this link to view Yvonnette O'Neal speak at the GCTS CUME Chapel: https://www.youtube.com/watch?v=WKRN_XAvwHU&t=1s.

38. LeaAnn Pendergrass, host of *Uniting the Nations* and pastor of My Gathering Place International. Click this link to view LeaAnn interviewed on *Beauty for Ashes*—with Gemma Wenger 05-10-2017: LeaAnn Pendergrass, Pastor of *My Gathering Place International*, reminds us in a recent interview that "God is no respecter of persons" (Acts 10:34). Christians are called to imitate Jesus by sharing His love with everyone. LeaAnn shares Jesus' love with the down and out and the up and out. Her interview on Gemma Wenger's *Beauty for Ashes* is linked in this chapter as a reminder that God loves the stranger and calls for his people to do the same (Leviticus 19:34), https://www.youtube.com/watch?v=oL_p3N4p7Qw&list=PLR3LLLVoBrcWDAONDajLrvffv-rxICn9c.

39. Cal State Teach Preparation Program: https://www.calstateteach.net/.

students said in Spanish they proceeded once again to instruct me in Spanish during lessons that increased their cognitive ability to speak English. The role reversal was energizing to them. The teaching method was bilingual because bi-lingual teaching assistants filled in, in Spanish. I used a modified two-way immersion technique. As class progressed, a modified version of immersion began: I spoke more English as I saw the students' English proficiency improved.

One day I walked a kindergartener named Isabella to meet her mother at the gate of the school. She was unhappy, and I asked why. She said, "*Sólo habla español.*" I said, "I am speaking Spanish to you in my heart, but I am teaching you English." She said, "Okay" in English. She had not spoken English the entire time in the classroom, although she responded with understanding to instruction in English. This was the most success I ever had using the communicative method teaching Hispanic learners. Isabella and I resolved a cultural conflict. She was willing to give English a try because she was confident that English proficiency would not compromise the Hispanic identity she loved so much. I believe that she was beginning to glimpse that learning English would give her the opportunity to make a difference in the world with her Hispanic DNA.

Recently, I had the opportunity to interview my longtime friend and colleague, psychologist Indira Palmatier. I told her about Isabella. With great insight, Indira identified the language of the mother tongue as providing one of our first and most impressionable interactions with the world:

"From the mother tongue can come early discovery of personal power, the sense of having an effect on the world around us. So, what does it mean to relinquish this, in favor of the language of a dominant culture? Does the "at risk" student become more "at risk" when his/her primary language is supplanted with English and yet another vulnerability exposed? Disability, race, socioeconomic status, history of incarceration or acting out, all are positions of being at risk, being vulnerable. Coping with the factors that made the person at risk to begin with is already a pressure, and to add to it what seems like another demand may seem to be an overload. What interest could the student possibly have in giving up his/her primary tool of communication and power, exchanging it for halting syllables and stumbling words in a foreign language?

The meaning attached to learning a new language must incorporate a personal value to the student. Many at risk students, already identifying themselves as being rejected by the dominant culture one way or another, could see "knocking on the door" to be let in through language as hopeless so without worth. First and most salient, I believe, then, is to explore the meaning of what it is to learn a new language, what does this signify?

Does learning English and being expected to embrace it in daily life represent leaving behind a lifetime of familiar colorful sounds and intonations? Is there an undercurrent feeling of disloyalty in some basic pervasive way? It makes sense to me.

Growing up as an immigrant in England in the 1950s and early 1960s, I experienced the value ascribed to accents. As a child I remember a continuous mild dread that came with feeling "one down" to the dominant society. One aspired to being as much like the "upper crust" as possible, with accents that, today, sound like speech impediments. If you had that accent the world opened up to you. If not, you could expect to be relegated to the lower echelons, your footsteps barely heard. Could there not be some vein of resentment at this pressure?

So, the question is What to do with a possible, almost organic, resistance to the very idea of changing something so ingrained as a language with all its nuances and nurturing. One could start right there. Questions such as "What are some important parts of your own language? What are things your mother said to you that you still remember? Please say these out loud in your mother tongue. How do you carry them with you? What do you feel when you hear your own language versus struggling to make yourself understood in another? (powerless, stupid, disregarded, an irritation?)". The longer the description the better—don't be afraid, just stay present, stay patient. The concept of "join and lead" begins to come alive. 'Besides the obvious, that it will help you get along in this society, how else might it be useful to learn English in a way you haven't thought of before? And, if that happened, then what else could happen? After that what else could open up for you personally? Who else could benefit? How? How would your identity change, who would you then be? Don't accept monosyllabic answers, express your faith that the students have the answers already within them. Eventually, with this line of reasoning one looks for "freedom" as the ultimate answer. And everyone wants freedom!

Important in goals to strive to reach is to listen as long and as deeply as one can. Only after all is "emptied out" is the receiver open to a new approach, a new possibility. At that point, when the goal is clear and bright, beautiful and beckoning, the teacher holds a precious hope for the future.

Eyes yield a small sparkle and dreams start to shape themselves in a touchable way.

The group setting where students have become privy to each other's deeper thoughts helps with trust and a common sense of wanting everyone to succeed. Students are more likely to help each other as well as reach out to others for help. The safety of the closeness opens up learning, opens up the world. One is not alone in this hurdle."[40]

FINAL THOUGHTS

The New International Version of the Bible translates Deuteronomy 32:2 as follows: "Let my teaching fall like rain and my words descend like dew, like showers on new grass, like abundant rain on tender plants" (NIV). I like both translations, but, as an Athanasian Scholar, I pray this song of Moses in Elliott's Version: "Everything that comes down from the 'Father of lights' is handed on by one heavenly messenger to another, until it falls upon the heart of man, in just that form in which he can best receive it." [41] In a recent interview, my fellow Athanasian Scholar Wilma Faye Mathis Owens explained to me her understanding of the importance of prayer for students:

"The privilege to teach is one of my heart's desires. So, when the Lord opened an opportunity I accepted without hesitation. You may wonder what has this to do with students? Well, everything. I have studied hard, learned from some extraordinary teachers, and have developed a passion to seed back into the lives of other students. The first thing I assure my students is that I will walk alongside you, be there to help you to organize, get through assignments, and brainstorm. But most of all, I will lift you up and call your name in prayer, asking that God will anoint and illuminate the faculty of your minds, until you gain a better understanding now and in your own continued studies. In the modern and this post-modern day, men and women have faced a lot of stress at work, home, ministry, and in school. But I am there to remind the students that Christ is the source of their strength, refreshment, and peace, and to remember: 'Whatever

---

40. Indira Palmatier, EdD, MFT, interview by email, May 23, 2017. View Indira caring for elephants at the Ran-tong Save & Rescue Elephant Centre: https://youtu.be/YANE-EeZw1U?list=PLR3LLLVoBrcWDAONDajLrvffv-rxICn9c.

41. Deuteronomy 32:2 (KJV). Bible Hub, "Ellicott's Commentary for English Readers," lines 2–4.

you do, do it enthusiastically, as something done for the Lord and not for people.'" (Col.3:23)

CONCLUSION

Each year, along with extraordinary Athanasian Scholars like Wilma Faye Mathis-Owens, I teach English Language Learners theology in the form that they can best receive it. In this chapter, I discussed the successful use of bilingual instruction, a communicative approach, creating a low stress environment and a happy mistake zone, strong teacher/ student eye contact, modified immersion, kinesics, modeling, repetition, role reversal, singing and finger play, tracing as a high sensory method to learn sight words, visual approach which encourages students to express what is near to their hearts. I also noted these strategies were handed down to me in texts from experienced teachers of English Language Learners as I completed courses in education for a California State Teaching Credential and from friends who are presently engaged in teaching English Language Learners as I continue to be myself. Now, I am passing them on to you, the reader.

By the end of each course I help teach, I am grateful for these strategies that helped my students learn, but my heart gives thanks to God who faithfully answers my prayer for supernaturally empowered aptitude for learning for each student. The look of understanding in the students' eyes, the pride in their accomplishments as a result of the extent of their efforts, and the joy they experience in the process of acquiring understanding are the greatest rewards to me for teaching theology to English learners. As a teacher, I am blessed as my students are blessed.

Chapter Seven

Dialogical Teaching in the Digital Age

DEAN BORGMAN

WHAT IS DIALOGICAL TEACHING. . .AND WHO AM I?

DIALOGICAL TEACHING MIGHT BE called relational teaching. And relational teaching may call for biographical disclosure. In fact, I think effective teaching begs biographical disclosure. That greatest of teachers, Jesus, continually stressed—especially to his critical objectors— the importance of his own identity and from where he had come. As a teacher appropriately shares her or his background, context, and perspective, students (of all ages) will be more open to share their own stories. My emphasis in this chapter therefore stresses biographical and narrative contexts and examples.

God calls some to farming, some to art, some to carpentry, some to computer science, and others to medicine. I didn't know it, and even fought it for a while, but God was directing me toward education. As with much of my early life, I fell backwards into teaching through unplanned experiences. Before college, I helped with Daily Vacation Bible programs and Sunday school teaching (and some small youth group meetings). My study of Jesus in the Gospels, followed by involvement in a large youth program at Black Rock Church in Bridgeport, Connecticut, and then starting a Young Life club in New Canaan, CT in the 1950s, challenged me to gain and keep youthful attention if teaching was to occur.

Reaching out to gang members and drug addicts on the Lower East Side of Manhattan in the 1960s, and some work with the Street

Academy program in Harlem during the 1960s led me further into relational teaching. No "White Teacher" would otherwise have mattered in those situations.

Then, in the early 1970s, I found myself teaching graduate students at Gordon-Conwell Theological Seminary in Hamilton, Massachusetts. My practical theology and teaching about youth ministries could hardly compete with lectures from renowned and systematic theological scholars. If my classes were to work, I had to get into student lives, their backgrounds, their experiences, viewpoints, and feelings. Contrast with most other teaching styles proved to make dynamic sessions for some students. These students were refreshed by those professors who took a personal interest in them and built classroom discussion upon personal stories.

Teaching at Cuttington College in Nigeria and then at Daystar University in Nairobi, Kenya exposed me to important cross-cultural issues. Participation in the founding of, and teaching at, Gordon-Conwell's urban campus in the heart of Boston proved to be an even greater privilege and learning process. I was now teaching more adult learners with a variety of ethnicities. My race and class, and even my male gender, could prove a barrier for some critical students. To teach African, African-American, Caribbean-American, Haitian-American, Asian-American and other students with rich ethnic identities, many of whom were English Language Learners, I had much to learn before teaching became effective.

I began to realize the importance, in teaching/learning, of personal identity, the result of personal stories, and the power of such in a learning process. It also struck me, and sometimes my students, that their personal stories, feelings, basic opinions where their opinions had originated and, thus, the starting points for their learning. I realized that students don't just show up as individuals. Rather, students of all ages at all levels of education in fact, bring their families, their ethnicities, their gender (possibly in confusion), and their life experiences into class. Do I care and am I ready to deal with the complexities of such relationships? Do you wonder with me how theology can be effectively taught without reference to personal situations and feelings and without consideration of emotional intelligence, and especially, without reference to social justice and the common good?

HOLISTIC TEACHING

Has theological education lacked emphasis on the soul and a "theology of the heart?" Certainly, it is enjoyable and critically important to read, think, and teach theology. But, to some degree, Western Euro-American theology may have become trapped in its own rational limitations. Of course, thinking is part of believing, but it is not the whole story; feelings, intuitions, and presuppositions of the heart are part of the searching-for-truth process. Good elementary teachers realize what professors at undergraduate and graduate schools may overlook. Teaching deals with physical bodies, then emotions, the mind—and for those spiritually inclined— most importantly: the heart.

Two men went into the temple to pray (Luke 18: 9-13). The Pharisee was *thinking* about himself and God; the publican or tax collector *sensed* something deeper within about himself. . . and God. The Pharisee prayed from a self-centered mind, the sinner from a deep heart-felt sense of guilt before a holy God. I believe the Pharisee struggled for truth in his mind, while the sinner allowed hard truth to sink into his heart.

Jesus, the great teacher—perhaps as the disciples were having a theological argument about greatness in the kingdom—"called a little child over to sit among his disciples and said, 'I assure you that, if you don't turn your lives around and become like this little child, you will definitely not enter the kingdom of heaven.'" (Matt.18: 2-3, CEB) Can this have anything to do with our teaching and learning? Careful thought in learning and teaching is necessary and satisfying. But Jesus seems to be reminding us of an even deeper channel for truth. Holistic insights come from childlike humility and willingness to be taught.

Holistic teaching attempts to take into account all systems of the learners and the context of outside systems that affect their life and learning. Teaching becomes a triad among students, subject, and teacher. Our observation and evaluation of the teaching process seeks a proper balance among these three elements: interest and attention on the part of students, interest and excitement about the subject, and the instrumentality of the instructor as a catalytic facilitator.

RELATIONAL TEACHING

Martin Buber was one of the most influential religious and philosophical figures of the twentieth century. As my biographical introduction indicates, it has been rich experiences that shaped my teaching. I bring models of teachers and styles of different child and youth programs (like Young Life) into my classrooms. So, I don't claim the ideas of Martin Buber to have been a primary motivator and guide, nor do I claim expertise in interpreting his profound work.

In fact, it was a TV clip in an airport that gave me special incentive to relate with special intensity with as many students as possible. The interview was with one of the world's greatest masseuses—asking the secret of her success and of her training of others. Her reply: "I myself, and I teach those I train to see the body on the table as the most important body in all the world at that time." Ahead of the class topic at the time, and before all my personal concerns, I want the student asking me a question, or being asked a question by me, or even one not paying attention at all. . .I want that student, at that time, to be my primary concern.

Each person may have a unique impression and interpretation of Buber's *I and Thou*, a basis for his dialogic philosophy and spirituality. In my own opinion, his reaction to European rationalism and rationalized theology, his study of the Bible, his commitment to Hasidism, and so much more led him to stress the importance of a whole person interacting with a whole person in a present moment, each growing and benefitting from an experience that cannot go on beyond that striking encounter. Buber is writing about how human beings approach existence; here I am narrowing that focus as to the manner in which teachers and students, student and students, can interact. Such mutual meeting or encounter can be rather mystically in the present. Buber writes: The primary term I-Thou can only be spoken with the whole being.[1]

I-It relationship, on the other hand, ". . .has no present, only the past. Put in another way, insofar as a man rests satisfied with the things that he experiences and uses, he lives in the past, and his moment has no present content. He has nothing but objects."[2]

The fullness of Buber's dialogic encounter points to the power of love in teaching relationships. There have been teachers who loved students

1. Buber, *I and Thou*, 3.
2. Ibid, 12–13.

because they could not love themselves—sometimes not even other adults. This points us to the dynamic triad of the Hebrew *Shema*. Transcendental love from the divine allows us to love ourselves fully and with such love to love our neighbor (or student) as ourselves.

Love is an important aspect of teaching and learning. Love involves, but is not essentially about, analysis. Love is the experiencing of another human being, as a human being who can contribute to our being, our growth, and welfare. True love accepts and cares for another holistically; such love does not dissect preferred parts of the beloved and is not highly conditional, using love as a means to another end. True love is patient and persistent. We will come to the fullness of love and teaching in our final section.

TWO-DIMENSIONAL DIALOGIC
TEACHING IN A DIGITAL AGE

The digital age has changed everything: the brain structure and functioning of emerging generations, the style of relationships and communication, the way students learn. Some contrasting generational and cultural illustrations come to mind. When I was a young high school teacher, a more experienced faculty member gave me this advice: "Throw enough mud on a wall and some of it will stick." His idea was that we are throwing knowledge at students, and they may get some of it as they are able. This is far from dialogical teaching.

My colleague and I teaching in Africa would come into the classroom and find most students sitting with notebooks. . .waiting for facts and principles from us who were supposed to know more, despite cultural differences. Truth was to be deposited into their notebooks. It took time and exercises to introduce interactive learning. How excited they became when stretched, often with difficulty, to become agents of learning themselves.

Young people, and older ones too, have all the world's knowledge just a click away. They are used to gaining such information in seconds and moving on to their next interest, need, or question. They want to discover truth with us rather than having it thrown at them by us.

Dialogic teaching involves talk between teacher and student and to some degree between students and students under the influence of the teacher. Excessive monistic teaching, lecturing, or long stretches of explanation can miss educable moments and opportunities. Dialogic teaching seeks the applicability of the subject to the student's present and future life; it also receives student "common-sense" perspective on the topic.

Dialogic teaching uses complex, rather than simple matter of fact, questions: questions that beg serious reflection and pondering of previous experience and knowledge. According to Robin Alexander, who has been studying dialogic teaching from the early 2000s, it requires:

- Interactions which encourage students to think, and to think in different ways,

- questions which invite much more than simple recall,

- answers which are justified, followed and built upon rather than merely received,

- feedback which informs and leads thinking forward as well as encourages,

- contributions which are extended rather than fragmented,

- exchanges which chain together into coherent and deepening lines of enquiry,

- discussion and argumentation which probe and challenge rather than unquestioningly accept,

- professional engagement with subject matter which liberates classroom discourse from the safe and conventional,

- classroom organization, climate, and relationships which make all this possible.[3]

Such goals for teaching can produce satisfied students who look forward to further learning experiences and classrooms that can become communal in a mutually beneficial sense.

THREE-DIMENSIONAL TEACHING: THEOLOGICALLY UNDERSTOOD

Good teaching can be dialectical and two-dimensional as we have seen. Christians can be good public-school teachers, and we can also learn much from secular educators. But when good, two-dimensional, horizontal education adds a vertical, three-dimensional feature, it approaches the world's

3. Alexander, "Dialogue Teaching," lines 8–16.

longing for Truth within the support of a Beloved Community. Our God is, in fact, three dimensional (to the limits of our understanding). We don't worship a one-dimensional God, but God in Three Persons, perfect Holism, perfect Being, perfect Family, perfect Community, and the model for all that is right and good.

When God's loving parenthood, the grace-bestowing model of Jesus our Lord, and the sweet influence of the Holy Spirit enters into a learning situation, a blessedness fills all hearts and learning flourishes for the common good.

EXTRAORDINARY TEACHERS AND LEARNING

Extraordinary teachers make for extraordinary students and learning. Extraordinary teachers seek extraordinary wisdom throughout their lives and teaching careers. There seems, biblically, to be three steps in such a quest:

1. Wisdom is the principle thing; therefore, get *wisdom*.

2. Do not be wise *in your own eyes*, fear the Lord and depart from evil.

3. The fear of the Lord is *the beginning of all wisdom* (Proverbs 4:7, 3:7, 9:10 NKJV)

The extraordinary teacher is often an extraordinary follower of Jesus Christ. Such followers put themselves in the position of our Great Teacher's interns as He called them together and said:

"Whoever wants to be first must be least of all and the servant of all." Jesus reached for a little child, placed him among the Twelve, and embraced him. Then He said, "Whoever welcomes one of these children in my name welcomes me; and whoever welcomes me isn't actually (or not just) welcoming me but, rather, the one who sent me." (Mark 9:35b-37, CEB)

Extraordinary teachers in the Jesus-teaching tradition know it is more blessed to give than to receive and that genuine giving is its own reward though often expressed through grateful students. This tradition remembers the last conversation between Peter and his exalted rabbi, the risen Lord. Soon to ascend, Jesus seemed to pester his recent denier, yet the one chosen to be "the Rock" and leader of the first church, with this penetrating question, "Peter, do you love me?" In response to Peter's repeated and agonized, "Yes, Lord, you know it to be so" The Teacher mandates a motto, driving all of us who teach, "Feed my lambs, Care for my Sheep, Feed my Sheep." [4]

When all is said and done, the most effective teachers won't be remembered primarily for their teaching. They will be remembered primarily as the kind of person they were and how they affected and influenced students and how they brought students together in community.

Finally, good teaching proceeds through teachers opened to continued growth, to new ideas to all kinds of students, and to the amazing operations of the Spirit of God. The overflowing love of God our Father, and Grace and example of Our Lord Jesus Christ, with the healing and growing presence of the Holy Spirit are the components that bring education to full fruition. Extraordinary teaching is, above all, to the praise and glory of God.

4. John 21:17.

Chapter Eight

English Language Learners as Pacesetters

VIRGINIA WARD

THE BOSTON CAMPUS OF Gordon-Conwell Theological Seminary, also known as CUME (Center for Urban Ministerial Education), serves many multi-ethnic students who are English-Language Learners (ELL). I call them pacesetters. Webster defines a pacesetter as someone who sets the pace at the beginning of a race or competition, sometimes in order to help another runner break a record. A second definition describes a person or organization viewed as taking the lead or setting standards of achievement for others.[1] Many of our ELL students are setting the pace for their families, their ministries and the communities they serve by pursing a theological education.

Pacesetters have a way of thinking that is different from others who just want to keep up, lag behind, or don't want to be in the race at all. I have witnessed students from various ethnic communities taking risks, sacrificing everything to gain an education in the United States. Often these students desire to return to their countries after graduation to bless and change their communities. Others remain for a season in order to practice the learning and perfect the models so that they can take them back tested. Some choose to relocate fully to the United States with their families. All of these scenarios are plausible with ELL.

Often the students are not reluctant to learn English, but do not want to associate with the culture that accompanies the language. The desire to

---

1 Merriam-Webster, "Pacesetter."

keep the foundation stones of their native land generally comes to a head when confronting the American culture, since learning the language brings to the forefront the necessity of learning the culture. In the classroom setting, students learn the nuances of the English language that go beyond grammar and phonetics. Real church and family situations are shared by the students searching for answers from the professor, their classmates and from the scriptures.

As an alumnus and now a professor of CUME students, over the years I have found that our ELL can be described in one of three category types: the senior pastor, the youth worker, and the lay leader. By reviewing these examples of faith and perseverance, we can glean lessons from the CUME urban environment. After the student types have been identified, I will offer some recommendations for engagement.

"Pastor Sam" is a Haitian born pastor leading a congregation of first generation Creole—speaking members who have given birth to American-born English-speaking children. His heart is still with his country, yet he seeks to build his family and ministry with the resources of America. Initially, Pastor Sam appears to be a bit reserved, observing his classmates and providing limited responses in a group setting. Once Sam was given an opportunity to share his story, his personality and joy of community sprang forth. Full of wisdom and eager to learn, he is not afraid to ask probing questions of the instructor and classmates.

Green to the American culture, many of his thoughts regarding ministry are centered on concerns for the Haitian family and the traditions of the Haitian church. He desires to influence leaders who will influence parents and the faith community to influence the future of the next generation with a message that mobilizes them to love God and serve others.[2] He recognizes the wrestling match between language and culture and views it as paramount to the success of the Haitian family in America. He seeks the preservation of his language, balanced with a clear understanding of enough English to navigate the classrooms and community he is called to serve.

Though he yearns for growth, he maintains a reluctance to change anything that could make this possible. The fear of becoming "American" causes him to cling to the familiar ways of doing things, especially the language. Pastor Sam likes to use phrases in Creole followed by "I don't know how to say this in English." His peers try to help him interpret the Haitian experience into American culture through the English language,

2 Joiner, *The Orange Strategy*, 19.

but inevitably something is lost in the translation. The language barrier is also visible in his written assignments especially when Pastor Sam struggles to relay his thoughts on paper.

"Youth Worker Maria" serves in a large Latino church in the greater Boston area. Her husband carries the title of the youth pastor; however, Maria actually shoulders the bulk of the responsibilities of the youth group. Due to the theological stance her denomination has held on to regarding women in ministry her status remains void of a title. She is concerned about the views of leadership after she completes the Master of Divinity, granting her a higher degree than her husband holds.

Maria has done well navigating the English language because she communicates with the youth of the church in English. She adapts quickly to the unspoken meanings behind many of the examples given in class and is able to assist other Latino/a ELL. Because of her connection to the youth, she feeds her husband information and bridges the two generations in the congregation. The youth services are held in English; however, the main services are held in Spanish. Maria, along with the youth, would like to see a service in English but doubt it will happen anytime soon.

The classroom for Maria is like a test kitchen. She bounces her ideas off the other ethnic groups and finds common ground in the discussions about the generation gaps in her congregation. Another discovery made in class concerns the gender issue in ministry. She was pleasantly surprised when women and men from other ethnic communities shared similar stories of women not being allowed to hold leadership positions. "I thought it was just me" was retorted by voices of her generation, some in agreement and others in disagreement. Maria's written work is not on the same level as her verbal skills in class. She has a degree of difficulty expressing her ideas in English and, on one occasion, she wrote a paper in Spanish and had a friend translate it prior to submission.

"Lay Leader Peter" is a member of the Chinese-American church and very active in ministry. He is concerned about the level of isolation in the Chinese church and its distancing from other Asian churches. An accomplished business man, Peter seeks a seminary education to sharpen his biblical skills and become a greater asset to the ministry. In class, he connects with the other Asian students and shares resources with them readily.

His posture in class is similar to Pastor Sam's, observant and reserved. In the first few classes he only shared in small groups but seemed very attentive. It was only after hearing the professor give the disclaimer that "all students have permission to share in class" did he and his other colleagues begin to share in the large group setting. The wisdom of years and experience were evident in his responses. Peter's written skills were close to his verbal skills; however, it was clear that the paper was written by an ELL.

As Peter revealed the world of Chinese-Americans, some Korean students felt comfortable sharing their lives with the class. Common ground was discovered not only in the Asian community but across the African-American, Caribbean, and Latino communities. The tapestry created by ELL covers the globe and should not be taken lightly.

Seminary classes are great learning labs for ELL students. The mastery of the professor coupled with the combination of the varied student cultures creates a unique environment of understanding. My recommendations for persons studying or teaching in ELL seminary environments are as follows:

- Allow the students in the classroom to shape the learning of each class member through group projects. The professor can be viewed as the facilitator of learning, not just the sole source in the classroom. Some students can benefit from the expertise of those sitting next to them, especially if they are more advanced ELL students.

- Clear definitions of terms and meanings are necessary to level the playing field for the ELL. It is not enough to state a term. Each ethnic group brings its own definition of words and things Americans assume are common knowledge. Taking the time to make explanations can go a long way with an ELL.

- Increase the ethnic IQ of the class and the professor beyond just food and music. As America continues to unveil the multiple ethnic communities already living in its neighborhoods, it behooves us to spend time learning other cultures. This makes a richer environment and equips every tribe, nation, and tongue to be able to learn within their native perspective and ultimately to share the gospel freely.

- View the writing assignments through the lens of culture. Once I read the papers of my students in their voice, I found translating their examples much easier. If I attempted to view their thoughts through my American lens, the void was great.

For a number of months now I have watched two women walk up and down our street as a part of their exercise plan. While one kept a steady, brisk pace (the pacesetter) the other one had to run sometimes to keep up, often passing but then becoming passed again by her friend. She never stopped or gave up. I'm sure at some point she complained under her breath—or worse—to others, "Why doesn't she just slow down? She always has to be upfront!" or even, "Why am I doing this?" It doesn't take all that!" This woman did not choose to give up, maybe she complained, but she kept on working and trying to catch up, trying to understand. Now, when you look at both of them, they are both healthy and you see the weight loss on BOTH of them, not just the one who kept the steady pace.

ELL can be misunderstood, sometimes talked about, and perhaps not liked, even hated by some. Throughout the academic process over the years, they develop thick skin and set their faces as flint, remaining focused on their goals. Each class, each learning experience provides another opportunity for God to give them hinds' feet enabling them to climb on slippery places while they keep moving, keep leaping. As we intentionally equip ELLs, it will require some changes in our seminary processes, however the body of Christ will truly be equipped together if we allow the pacesetters to keep us moving.

Chapter Nine

Intentional Teaching [1]

WILLIAM DAVID SPENCER

Each year, I tell my multicultural students how delighted I am to be teaching them and, particularly, how much I honor them for braving the learning of English. I am not exaggerating when I tell them that I firmly believe that, if I were not born a native speaker of English, I'm not sure I would have been able to master this tongue as well as they do.

The way I could illustrate the explanation of what they have accomplished in mastering English to whatever degree they have is to point out they have managed to negotiate not just the trekking of the wild terrain of simply one new language, but they have descended into a deep, rich jewel mine of precious word gems from a number of rich veins of languages. Or, I might tell them that, when they entered the realm of English, they didn't stumble upon a simple campfire cookout but arrived instead at a four-star restaurant buffet table overflowing with rich delicacies from a number of international cuisines.

English is, after all, less a tongue in itself than a composite of languages built on the root dialects of the ancient Germanic tribes of Angles, Saxons, and Jutes, as these melded with the native Gaelic of the primal Celts when they were cut off together on that island by wars and plagues to simmer and

---

1. This chapter is dedicated to Dr. Sylvia Feldman, formerly of Rutgers University, New Brunswick, New Jersey, who expertly demonstrated instruction oriented by acknowledging individual differences. The chapter is an adaptation of an article published in http://www.gordonconwell.edu/resources/Africanus-Journal.cfm from a presentation I recently gave to the students of Gordon-Conwell's Africanus Guild PhD support program.

then be infused with a heady seasoning of French and Breton and Old Norse by the Norman invasion by my namesake William the Conqueror, a descendant of the Vikings, in A.D. 1066. Meanwhile, this stew pot of languages had been picking up more than a pinch of spicy cognates (that is, loan words) from Greek and Latin and whatever else those who happened to be invading its shores were speaking. While the current natives were fending off one Roman general or another with an eye on waging a successful campaign to bolster a future bid for emperor or repulsing whatever would-be conqueror who happened to be plundering the neighborhood at the time, the end result was more and more words and new constructions creeping like mole spies into the language to settle in and subvert it once again.

Flash forward a couple millennia and its present heir, contemporary American English, is like a five-course dinner to ingest from a global kitchen for any English Language Learner (ELL). Our alphabet's common letter names, of course, are useless in guiding people to read, or, in our spelunking metaphor, we might say they're slag, or in our culinary one, indigestible. For example, the letter B, whose name is pronounced "Bee", does nothing to tell an English Language Learner how to pronounce its actual sound in spoken usage, because that is "buh". C is a non-functional, vestigial organ, mimicking S and K and doing nothing on its own—that slacker should be fired from the alphabet and sent packing. Past tenses are chaotic. Sometimes, we teach students to add "ed" endings, as in "I look" to "I looked." Sometimes, we teach word substitutions as in "I go" expressed in the past as "I went." Sometimes we just mispronounce a word in order to do both functions, as in "I read," "I read." Figure that one out! And what about plurals? Sheep is the singular and—wait a second!—sheep is the plural? It's enough to make an ELL want us all to switch to Spanish, or Greek, or Hebrew, or Kikuyu—or any language that has a better sound-symbol correlation.

This is where I thank God for a Congregational missionary named Frank Laubach. This genius brilliantly conceived of a program that mounted the hurtles of English by creating what English lacks—a coordinated sound/symbol system. What Laubach did was make a picture out of each letter of the English alphabet, indicative of that letter's sound. This sound-symbol correlation ensured that, when a student pronounced the letter the picture was indicating, e.g. a bird to depict the letter B, the English Language Learning student wasn't derailed by the letter name sound "Bee," but was being guided by the actual pronunciation of the English word "bird" sound-wise, which is, in reality, something like *buherduh*. If you sound it out rapidly, you'll see how it works. The Reverend Laubach was making certain the letter sound (not the misleading letter name) was the first sound uttered. When I taught literacy classes, I would drill my students, and they would reply, "What's the letter name?" "Bee!" What's the picture?" "Bird!" "What's the sound?" "Buh!" "What's the sound?" "Buh!" "What's the sound?" "Buh!" What are you going to think about when you see this letter?" "Bird!" "So what sound are you going to say?" "Buh!" Over and over again, creating a sound/symbol correlation to construct in each student's mind the building blocks of reading letter by letter by letter by a sound/symbol correlation.

Frank Laubach also added in extra symbols we need but don't have in English, for example the first sound in "shop." English spelling uses the alphabet letters "SH" to begin the word "shop," but they don't help anyone discover the sounding out of this word. Honestly—think about it—how exactly does "sssssshaaaa" make the first sound in the word "shop?" Take a moment and make the "S" sound, "s-s-s." You're curling your tongue and forcing air over it in a sibilant sounding like a snake hissing. For "ha-a-a," you have to open up your mouth cavity widely and force air in the cavern between the drawn-down tongue and the roof of the mouth. But the sound for "Shop" is done in the front of the mouth, streaming air over the turned-down tip of the tongue and the drawn-down roof of the mouth, all forced forward through pursed lips. The ways these sounds are made are very different. The letter names "S" and "H" are worse than useless, they are completely misleading, if one is trying to teach ELL students to sound out the word "Shop" so that anyone can understand what they are asking and point them in the right direction to the local "Stop and S-S-S-h-a-a-op!" And, while we are listing our grievances, the "ti" "ha" "ē" letter name sounds don't help at all if someone is trying to make sound sense out of the word "the." How could the letter names sounded out as "ti-ha-ē" ever give an ELL any inkling how to sound out the word "the?" And, don't even try to teach them a correlation between the first sound in "Children," as misrepresented by "cee" "ha" (or is it "kee" "ha" a new ELL wonders. . .). It is mystifying how anyone ever learns to speak English with such a clash between the names of the letters in our alphabet and the actual phones into morphs that we use as we build words. What we need in English, of course, to solve the three examples I just gave is the Shin symbol from Hebrew and the Theta symbol from Greek, and I settled for the "chu" sound in the Spanish alphabet, because it, at least, is featured as a separate letter. But until we get new symbols or change our letter names to their actual sounds, Frank Laubach's picture substitutions to invoke the sounds at the sight of the letters works well in my experience in teaching new English language readers to read.

Once I was armed with this new paradigm, due to training as a Laubach literacy teacher in the innovative program set up, developed, and supervised by the master teacher Sharon Darling in her pioneer literacy program under the auspices of the Jefferson County, Kentucky, Board of Education, basically targeting urban and mountain folk trying to survive in Louisville, Kentucky, the mystery of teaching English broke open for me. Practice, of course, is the tougher task master that yields experience. The burnout rate of a literacy teacher I was told in that day was a year and a half. After two years of my working in the program, Sharon, my boss, made me teaching coordinator for Jefferson County and I proceeded to set up and help run eight literacy and GED (high school equivalency) centers in all, continuing to teach and administer until my wife (now the Rev. Dr. Aída Besançon Spencer) graduated from Southern Baptist Theological Seminary with her doctorate in New Testament (which was why this New Jersey boy was in Louisville teaching in the first place), and she had the opportunity to respond to the call to go to (what my Mom called "God's Country" and I refer to as "the frozen north") Gordon-Conwell Theological Seminary's Hamilton, Massachusetts campus to teach New Testament. I brought this training and experience with me, adding on to what has now accumulated into fifty-one years of urban ministry, as you'll read in my bio sketch.

As I was when arriving in Louisville, once more a stranger, this time in Massachusetts, with nobody asking me to do anything, I realized, if I was ever going to complete my own education—this was the moment. So, I did my doctorate in Theology and Ancient Literature at Boston University School of Theology, working with two wonderful supervising scholars (both Lutherans at this Methodist school), Drs. Elizabeth Bettenhausen and Carter Lindberg. Within a year of arrival, just when I was starting my doctoral studies, I was asked to offer summer courses at Gordon-Conwell's Hamilton campus, so, while I taught and worked on my doctorate, I pursued my childhood goal of writing books, starting with the shrinking of my 827-page doctoral dissertation down to printable size. It became my first book, *Mysterium and Mystery: The Clerical Crime Novel* (dealing with fictional detectives from the Apocrypha on to the present day, who, when the police were baffled, stepped in with God's guidance and solved the crime. My interest centered on how God's great "mysterium," the revelation of profound good, had transformed into the secular righting of evil in popular culture). I was now entering a suburban-based scholarly life for the first time, though we did plant a storefront church in a neighboring city and that kept us urban-focused.

And then all that past experience in educationally-oriented city ministry, particularly in New York with urban pastors, Newark with storefront pastors, and Louisville with literacy students kicked back in. Nine years after I'd been teaching desultory courses on the Hamilton campus, I was invited by then Boston campus dean Dr. Efrain Agosto to teach Systematic Theology 1 and I arrived at Gordon-Conwell's multicultural Center for Urban Theological Education (CUME). I was back in the city. At the present date of writing (Winter, 2017) I am still teaching courses in theology for the Boston Campus/CUME, some twenty-five years later. So, what did I find myself adapting from my background to help me teach my multicultural classes of urban-ministry oriented saints from a myriad of different cultural backgrounds, many of whom are English Language Learners? This chapter will detail how Laubach Literacy and parallel GED training, fused with urban teaching experience when I was back with New York Theological Seminary, and street ministry experience before all of it, helped me negotiate the teaching of my multicultural classes and be useful to my students.

ADAPTING A METHODOLOGY THAT ENCOURAGES STUDENTS TO LEARN AND NOT DROP OUT, DISCOURAGED

Over the years, I have come to realize that teaching begins with a compound question that I find myself asking continually: what am I doing here and how do I measure my success?

What I am doing here is serving the Lord, so I measure my success by what pleases the Lord.

How am I serving the Lord? I have been given the task of moving students ahead in their mastery of the field of theology and their ability to apply the findings of that field to ministry. My calling is to take each student from the spot of learning where she or he is presently located when enrolling in my class and move every one forward in each one's understanding of and ability to perform successfully within the subject matter in a way so responsible and yet relevant that what I teach on Wednesday night can be preached from a city pulpit on Sunday morning, as well as applied to a variety of ministry situations throughout the week. So, I please the Lord when, by style (model) of instruction, choice of content, and instructional methodology, I maximize my positive results. (And to all my former students, this is my subtle topical thesis statement, in case you are searching for one.)

So, when I am able to do so, I begin with the learning environment, attempting to turn my classroom itself into an instructional tool. This I brought over from my years teaching literacy where a static classroom was set up with every conceivable aid from books to machines secured in the same places and available in turn week after week. However, one obstacle I continually faced once I arrived in Boston was that I could not make my classroom a total learning environment as I could when I was teaching in a literacy or GED center because I am not the sole teacher using my classrooms, since these are held in shared ownership and revolving space. For the first decade, I mainly taught in churches: a Spanish Methodist church in Chelsea, a Chinese Church in Brookline, several African-American Churches in Dorchester and Roxbury, a Cambodian Church in Mattapan, a Haitian Church in downtown Boston, the former funeral home in Jamaica Plain we used as our office center—wherever the students were, we teachers went there. Even today, when we have our own building in Roxbury, any number of classes use the same classroom I do, so it is not just a theology lab, so as to say, but it serves Old Testament classes, church planting classes, New Testament survey classes—whatever class is large and needs a big classroom.

Therefore, I have had to move from a physical to a more spiritual/emotional/intellectual environmental model built on a style of instruction and deportment hospitable to the students, in which each can feel a support and freedom that instigates and enhances learning.

STYLE OF INSTRUCTION

Creating such an environment these days begins before the class itself with an email welcoming students to the course, then arrival by myself through the endless snarl of Boston traffic sufficiently before class to welcome each student personally and handle each of their initial concerns from signing paperwork for late registrants, to allying fear that someone is too old to study, to handling concerns that the English of a sizable portion of the students is not good enough to survive the rigors of theological study, and on and on. Each of these issues can be negotiated by me or my associate teaching scholars on the first day. Since some of my graduates work with me through several courses in a given semester, if students are familiar with them, they feel safe and welcomed. All the students can tap into any resources they need, not only from the teaching staff, but especially from our gracious library staff, who join us in coaching the students in theological writing tirelessly year and after year, helping any who ask to handle written assignments in partnership with us. Our campus library in the basement of our building is one of our key safety nets.

Next, I view the classroom itself as a multi-level learning environment. In a single classroom, I try to be conscious to support at-risk students, value normally-paced students, and encourage advanced students, and, at the same time, train future staff.

Since my classes are six-weeks-intensive classes, comprised of students from many ethnic and national backgrounds, and these classes average these days between thirty to sixty adult students of varying degrees of English facility, I need to recruit teaching associates (under a program I created of enlisting outstanding graduates of my classes whom I dubbed Athanasian Teaching Scholars, in honor of Athanasius, the great North African defender of Nicaea's orthodox creed). I recruit my graduates who are adept in various languages and preferably equipped with second language teaching skills. This way I use the opportunity to train the next wave of seminary professors.

In a multicultural class, I have the opportunity to look for the best and brightest potential teaching scholars who have demonstrated mastery of the subject matter from each of my ethnic constituencies, so I keep an eye on those excelling students who demonstrate expertise in a second language (mere ethnicity does not automatically ensure language proficiency), because they will be accessible to ELLs from their particular primary language and, at the same time, will be sensitive to the challenges the ELLs are facing. For my classes this past semester, I was blessed with Athanasian teaching scholars and a Byington Scholar (an undergraduate the school hires) from Korean, Haitian, African-American, and Hispanic backgrounds. In addition, our school's long-term librarian, a former Athanasian Teaching Scholar from years past with a background in secondary school education, works with a few students with learning disabilities who have been identified as such in her initial required class on theological research and writing. This way, every student is being addressed by one of the four or five of us. This is one of my several attempts to individualize learning in a large classroom.

Now, about the Athanasian Teaching Scholars, I want to stress they are not simply teaching assistants doing graduate work apportioned out among the professors. My wife and I set some of our tithe aside (since our Boston campus operates on a low budget, due to the half price cost of classes), so that, as I track the performance in class of each student, I can identify at graduation those outstanding ones who have distinguished themselves in their class work, evidenced passion about theology, sensed a calling to teach, demonstrated discipline in their work, and have well developed personal skills. These days, I try to build in moments when I discuss individually with my teaching scholars topics such as how to build a syllabus, how to interact with students, how to grade, how to set a teaching style and make class content choices that will help make their teaching successful. I have also created detailed grading guides that all of us use, so grading is the same no matter who does it. Students don't have to run between us to see who is the easiest grader, as students might be tempted to do. To make the system work, students may submit different assignments to different ones of us, but they may not give the same assignment to more than one of us. As it is, given the size of our classes and the rigor with which we work with them in six-week stints, we average a thousand drafts between all of us in a three or four course semester. Sometimes, we receive up to eight revisions each of the two papers we assign, particularly from ELLs who want to master written expression and get it all right.

My wife occasionally hires her own Athanasian Scholars as she teaches New Testament on the Hamilton campus, though not at the frequency I do, which is two or three Athanasian Scholars per course on the Boston campus. Several other professors in the Boston campus have also begun to hire Athanasian Scholars of their own.

In addition, part of our vision is to set up opportunities for higher education for our teaching scholars. As a result, my wife established Gordon-Conwell's Master of Theology degree, followed by a program called the Africanus Guild (named for the great early church scholar and apologist Julius Africanus), which is a PhD support program that partners our school with two external research doctoral programs (presently with North-West University in South Africa and London School of Theology). Our Gordon-Conwell supervising professors in the Africanus Guild serve as partners with the supervisors from these external programs of the degree-granting schools.

After Athanasian Scholars complete their first-year tenure, we hold a dinner at our home each year where we honor that year's scholars with a plaque of appreciation and a copy of Athanasius's *On the Incarnation* and induct the next year's scholars with one piece of advice offered by each past Athanasian Scholar attending. (We also have a speaker and invest in a book from that speaker free to every family attending.) Further, we also intercede for those who enroll as PhD candidates as opportunities arise to teach at our school. While roughly 50 percent of my Athanasian Scholars have taught courses for our Boston Campus, others have gone on to teach for other seminaries, colleges, and universities, one even becoming a dean at a Bible college the year after he graduated. I myself rehire many of these scholars as years go by, so in each class there are new as well as seasoned Athanasian Teaching Scholars and the new inductees can continue to get advice on the job from the veterans as well as from me. While sometimes I assign students to Athanasian Scholars who are specialists in areas in which particular students need help to succeed, normally all students pick the staff person with whom they want to work. Also, the *Africanus Journal*, http://www.gordonconwell.edu/boston/africanusjournal,the free on-line journal we base in our Boston campus, my wife and I founded initially to provide a vehicle both for the professors in our Africanus Guild program and for our PhD students to publish book reviews and outstanding articles. The journal has since taken on its own astute readership and expanding field of excellent contributors, drawing at first on alumni, but now attracting articles from professors, pastors, and para-church leaders from other schools, ministries, and churches around the United States and throughout the world who share with us a high view of Scripture. We have also helped establish three book lines with Wipf and Stock, Publishers: the House of Prisca and Aquila Series, our Evangelical Egalitarian line which published the present volume you are reading, the Africanus Monograph Series, publishing outstanding dissertations, and Urban Voice, created by our esteemed colleague John Runyon, our school's gifted former administrator now with his brilliant Brazilian wife, Dr. Eliana Runyon (both of whom still teach for our campus), administrating the Massachusetts Institute of Technology (MIT) Sloan School of Management. All three book series, as well as the journal, are available to our Athanasian Teaching Scholars to publish any outstanding work (as they are to readers who share evangelical, egalitarian, biblical inerrantist convictions). Finally, we also established a study group, Other Voices in Interpretation, in the Evangelical Theological Society (ETS), to which, among other scholars, our doctoral students may submit their very finest work for possible presentation, as they may to ETS's other sections.

HOW IS ALL THIS FLESHED OUT IN CLASS?

Classes run Wednesday nights from 6:00 p.m. to 10:00 p.m. with a break at 8:00 p.m. After the break, in the second half of each first day class (I hold off so that all lost students will have found their way safely through Boston traffic), I spell out the assignments in the syllabus, which I have already posted on CAMS and which I have emailed several weeks before class begins to each enrolled student, so each has an e-copy, a hard copy, and the verbal explanation in great detail, since I take into account the fact that different students learn in different modes. I also blend in choice in the assignments. For example, in Systematic Theology 1, students are assigned a general topic: "Study One Attribute of God and Show How It Addresses One Problem Facing Your Church or Yourself (Something You Care About in Your Ministry)." They have the freedom to select the attribute of God they prefer to study and a related topic from a long list of suggestions I provide (the final two pages of which are drawn from original student idea contributions over the years), or to create their own combination of divine attribute and issue, subject to staff approval. Attributes and issues should, of course, relate (e.g., "God the Father and Fatherless Children," or "God Who is on the Side of the Widow and Orphan and Human Trafficking," or "The Lord of Hosts and the Problem of Whether or Not a Christian Should Serve in the Military (and, if so, in What Capacity?)," etc.). Topics have a wide range of application both personal and collective in scope. And the best results come when students select issues about which they care deeply. Then I outline for them what they need to do on each page of the paper (see Appendix #1). This assignment helps each student to begin doing theology, which in my view is applying the nature of God to the issues emerging from what God created. John Calvin in his opening insight in his *Institutes* observes, "Nearly all the wisdom we possess, that is to say, true and sound wisdom, consists of two parts: the knowledge of God and of ourselves.", or as I adapt this for my students: we know who we are when we know who God is.[2]

To help them out, my wife and I together have created sophisticated check lists for each of our courses that we call "cover sheets" with entries addressing each area of content and execution of the assignments for each of our classes, inspired by the high school equivalency [GED] checklist I

---

2. Calvin, *Institutes of the Christian Religion*, 35.

used to use when I ran several GED centers in Louisville (see Appendix #2 for a sample cover sheet).

Students do a first draft and hand the paper into me or to the Athanasian Teaching Scholar of their choice. I and the Athanasian Scholars follow the grading guides and mark the cover sheets so, as I noted, all students are graded by the same set of criteria no matter which of us works with them, but we also grade only for content, never for grammar, which I (and many of the Athanasian Scholars) fix on every paper without grading that aspect to help the students learn to communicate better in English writing. Athanasian Teaching Scholars themselves cannot give final grades, only I can do that as the professor of record, but Athanasian Scholars can and often do give interim grades to help students mark their progress in mastering the assignments. I do take these interim grades very seriously and, if a student chooses not to redo a final version—though that is rare—I regrade the last revision. If my grade differs from that of my Athanasian Scholar—an even rarer occurrence, since we all use the same system—I average the two grades together. I explain this to the students carefully. Grading has often been divisive between teacher and student, but this system puts the grade outside the relationship and, with so much staff, we are willing to guide them to redo and redo until they master the assignment and, thereby, master the content of the course. When I grade all final papers, I fix any remaining grammar errors as a final gift to the students to help them in their writing for their future classes.

So, students are encouraged to revise their papers all during the class, guided by the comments on the cover sheet and advice of the instructor with whom they are working, but they must hand in final revisions at the end. No revisions are accepted after the final class. (Otherwise, I remind them that, when the Second Coming of Jesus [the *Parousia*] takes place and, as we are rising to meet the Lord in the air [1 Thess. 4:17], there they will be, floating beside me, waving yet one more revision at me!) I also warn them repeatedly they also must never discard either earlier drafts or cover sheets but must hand each previous draft and noted cover sheet in with each new revision to have that redoing accepted. This way we don't have to keep re-grading papers over again from word one. We only grade the changes they made. This makes it all doable and also allows me never to close my rolls during the semester, so that anyone who wants to study with me can. The course is intensive, but this system makes it "theology without tears" (for Athanasian Scholars as well as students) as I assure them each year. I love theology and want them all to love it too. My system takes away the fear of a poor grade for the student, and the payoff for us teachers is that we have a mechanism in place to assure each one the maximum learning opportunity. Nobody is left baffled staring at a final paper with a single grade with no explanation of why they succeeded or failed. Everyone has become an active partner in his and her own learning. And all the teaching staff can rest at peace each night, knowing we've done our best to enable learning. This is the difference, I believe, between simply delivering lectures and actually teaching students content, while sharpening their scholarly skills so they can apply them effectively in future classes in which our safety net may not be in place.

Another way I build in individual attention for students is to schedule a seventh class for volunteer meetings on the Monday between the fourth and fifth class sessions (regular classes these days are four hours on six consecutive Wednesday evenings). According to our schedules, I and my Athanasian Scholars meet with as many students as wish to meet with us (I in the morning on the Hamilton campus and all evening at the Boston campus) and the Athanasian Scholars mainly during the day or in the evening (depending on each student's and each Scholar's availability) on the Boston campus, where the class is held. In the meetings, we can go over the students' paper assignments with them individually and discuss any theological topic of concern to them arising out of the class sessions. These meetings are not mandatory and those who feel confident in their work and that they are well served don't need to sign up.

Anyone who appears to be falling through the cracks, however, we attempt to intercept on the special interview day, when I particularly invite those not yet handing anything in by the fourth class to sign up to meet with one of us. Each week, of course, the Athanasian scholars invite students to email or call them and I invite students to call me by telephone during two sets of office hours each day (noon and late afternoon) on four days a week, or to leave a message at other times when I may return their calls.

All general course assignments are drawn from the heart of what I want students to learn in the class, so that, when a student succeeds on the paper assignment, the student has mastered the core content of the course. In the Theology 1 assignment, I want them to learn that the nature of God can be used as a hermeneutic (an interpreting tool) that answers all apologetic questions we face. Employing God's nature as a tool for interpretation, then, becomes the central theory on which all theology is done, becoming the foundational methodological tool for all three required theology classes. The reason this interpretive approach to the entire three-prong enterprise (interpretation, systematizing, application) of doing theology works is because we have been created in the image of God, so God's nature is central to who we are and, therefore, what we do. Every one of my classes (and, indeed, my own theologizing) is built on understanding God's nature as our central interpretive principle.

All successive lectures and class exercises in doing theology in all the rest of the courses I teach develop this approach, and it guides the way the topics of the study of God (theology) are organized, ordered for presentation, and presented.

DEPORTMENT IN CLASSROOM

Here are some of the practical ideas I employ for succeeding in the classroom:

1. This may seem like a strange subsection to include, but it's actually central to teaching. Back in 1968, when I was a college senior doing my practice teaching in a highly regarded local high school, I asked for advice to whomever would give it to me. One rather jaded veteran survivor told me, "I've got just one piece of advice to give you." He peered at me sternly from behind his desk and growled, "This was given to me by my supervising teacher and I've taken it to heart—and you should too!" I waited expectantly for the revelation to ascend (I was standing, not having been invited to sit). "Here it is," he snapped. "Always keep the little s.o.bs on their side of the desk." He glared a moment longer then nodded his head down toward the papers on his desk. The interview was over. I resisted the impulse to crawl out backwards, banging my head on the floor, as P.G. Wodehouse described his own dismissal from one editorial presence. I pondered this advice, since it came with no amplification, bestowed on me with the certitude of a universal truth, and I could see it was about maintaining power, related to the old adage of singling out the first student who steps out of line and creating an example to terrify the others into submission, so education could start.

   To me, however, from then until now, I've noticed that modeling sets the style that students will replicate when they move into their own positions of power. In secular schools, the goal is to create productive citizens, not power-hungry abusive bullies. In seminary, the goal is to train godly leaders, church pastors, para-church ministers, educators in churches and schools, missionaries, Christian book and periodical editors, informed lay leaders, administrators, street ministers, saints engaged in a variety of callings. If we treat them compassionately or callously, they will learn that model and that's how they will treat those in their charge.[3]

Years ago, I had a professor from a Christian Bible College in my class who stopped me at the end of the course and told me, "You've changed my whole view of teaching. I always saw teaching as a weeding-out process, getting rid of the dross that couldn't measure up. I see

---

3. One thought on this: I teach adults called to ministry. Pilgrim Church, the church my wife and I planted with mainly former students some thirty years ago and which we still help serve, is a storefront church serving a small city. Our parishioners are largely urban-based, and several are teaching in secular secondary school systems with adolescents in their classes from backgrounds of abuse, many of these being students with limited English proficiency (LEP) and with interrupted formal education (SIFE), forced, as they see it, into the school system because of their age. As a result, some of these arrive in class with multiple problems. Their response to their life situation is trying to live out the gangsta lifestyle. Prepared to do nothing else to survive, several are dealing drugs—on their own, completely out of control, and unresponsive to learning or to discipline. In one teacher's class, many of the other students are refusing to do any work, since they argue the rebellious ones don't and they get away with it. According to three of these teachers, all in different cities' schools, fights break out in class regularly. One told me she is terrified in class and learning has completely broken down. This is not a Hollywood movie where the hip teacher wins over the miscreants with several inspiring words and creative actions (often dealing with sports); this is real life. I think, especially in this last case, since her administration has not been responsive, but simply tells her to find a way to deal with this problem herself, I might explore the legality of hiring a specialist, a youth counselor or an off-duty policeman trained in dealing with youth to work with me in the classroom to help maintain order. Obviously, I would want to learn from veteran teachers what my options are for maintaining a learning environment, but the bottom line is no teacher who cares should have to endure a situation of terror or watch the class become disenchanted with learning and marginalized because of a usurped hostile turf war that puts everyone at risk. Lack of budget, of course, to hire supportive personnel is always the problem with schools in poor areas. Non-profits are always low budget, too. But, teachers who want learning to take place do need to take control of their classes' progress. That is their right. In my non-violent class of Christians with its segment of LEP students, hiring Athanasian Scholars is my solution, and, since the school budget can't pay the extra expense, we use our tithe to create the kind of class environment and assistance we and our students need to get the task done right. But the teachers at risk also need to have the freedom to be able to think and act effectively to ensure the best opportunity for their students to learn in a safe and supportive environment outside the box—especially if they're worried about a threat to themselves or one or more of their students ending up in one....

now what you're doing is very different. You gave me the opportunity to redo my paper over and over until I learned how to do it right from your comments. I never thought of that before—no professor ever did that for me before I took this class. It's grace in action. From now on, I'm going to let students redo their papers and teach them more gently." "Yes," I said, "you're educating the next wave of Christian leaders. Our job is to help them become more Christ-like." "I wish I could go back," he mourned. "I would do it all differently." "Me too," I commiserated. "I'd do a lot of stuff differently in my life. But all we can do is just change when we clue in and thank God for being so merciful to us." Teaching is more than simply delivering content. It is, indeed, modeling the grace God has given us in action.

2. Don't be afraid of your students. They may be older than you are. They may look different. They may even look initially frightening—some of them big, hairy, beetle-browed, a lot like a villain you recently saw in a classic 1940s gangster flick.

But, always remember that they all signed up to take your course. Thus, they want your approval. You hold their grade. So, let them know you want them to succeed. They will inevitably relax, if they know you are there to help them. These are, after all, all seminary students, so they must love God and sense God's calling, or they would not be in your class. If they are adults, chances are they are just as scared as you are—probably more so.

My mother, who was an award-winning saleswoman in the Macy's chain of department stores, used to tell me, "Everybody wants to feel important." I realized that is because everybody *is* important. God conceived of each of us before the foundations of the world and created us for this place at this time. So, I treat each student as called and precious. I determine beforehand that there are no Judases in my classes. Every one of them is my favorite, even those who are very different than I am and to whom, without an act of the will, I might not initially be drawn. However, before I even meet them, I determine to love them.

In our various prison ministries, my wife and I put into effect the strategy of treating each inmate as we wanted each to become, and, usually, each one strove to become that person in our eyes. So, we brought that strategy over from prison ministry to the classroom. I realized, if we could love each of the inmates as brothers in Christ (or, in one prison, sisters), we could easily love each of the seminarians as brothers and sisters in Jesus, too. Again, it is simply modeling grace in action.

3. Provide a support network: I try to pray for students, beginning before the class commences. I have supplied Athanasian Teaching Scholars to work particularly with the at-risk students and I have picked the Athanasian Scholars both for their theological prowess and their personal skills. I explain to students that potential teaching scholars must demonstrate an insatiable love and exceptional aptitude for the topic (in this case theology), along with a divinely gifted love for the students, manifested by strong personal skills, and a divinely-appointed pedagogical proclivity: in short, a clear calling by God to teach. All of these points are true, so telling them to the students not only builds trust in the students for working with the Athanasian Teaching Scholars, but also encourages them to strive to become one themselves. Goal-setting advertising pays off in evoking zeal and commitment.

4. Be sensitive to the customs and challenges of your students. I've learned that Korean ELLs are often unable to read cursive but can navigate print writing. Also, expect to return all their bows; it is disrespectful to stand there bewildered, gaping at them like we think they dropped a contact lens. Haitian students newly come to the USA may have been taught that all knowledge is common property, so they may reproduce material on the net without footnoting. What looks like plagiarism to the scandalized professor is not grounds for hauling them off to the academic disciplinary committee: it's a signal that they need to be taught to use quotation marks and footnotes before some lesser consciousness-raised teacher than you has them booted out of the program. Learn all their names. Names are important. Sometimes it takes the second or third class with a student to get the name fixed in my mind, especially since so many international names are unfamiliar to me. Sometimes, it takes many classes to pronounce a name correctly, but it is well worth the effort. Recognizing students individually honors them, affirms our valuing of them, and encourages them to perform at their best, which instigates learning. Each of our students is a precious child of God.

INTENTIONAL INSTRUCTION: MAKING IT ALL WORK

I hope that, if you only remember one thing from my chapter, it will be this: every second of class time is precious and therefore everything you do should be intentional—good teaching is not done by guesswork. I believe every part of our preparation and classroom behavior must be intentional, even our asides, most of which I write into my lecture notes before the class begins. Ninety-nine-point-nine percent of everything I am going to teach, confide, show, announce, or have my students do as a class exercise is already set in order before the class begins and is present in the huge notebook I lug into class the first day. (Systematic Theology 1 is now in two colossal notebooks.) And every year I revise and update my lectures before the semester begins to keep it all relevant. After twenty-five years teaching this particular version of Theology 1 and seventeen doing Theology 2 and 3 why am I still doing this?

All of us have been shortchanged by unprepared instructors who have entered the classroom talking randomly about their families, giving misleading multiple choice tests, belittling students, and mumbling, off the cuff, desultory thoughts about their disciplines rather than delivering well-structured lectures and conducting insight-producing exercises that together drive the kind of classes that help students progress, since those must be carefully constructed to move every student forward toward a workable understanding of each class's content and, thus, successful mastery of each course's objectives.

Many of today's students are internet-information-oriented. No topic need be boring—all are relevant to a technologically-oriented, post-modern audience, trying to retrieve what it can use from the past with the tools of the future. Liberal arts students are now able to see the relevance of calculus, as they may not have done some fifty years ago, and future engineers realize the need for sharpening communication skills. In this mixing of the disciplines, there are no boring topics, only boring teachers. Don't be one.

On secular topics, failed courses are lamentable (and sometimes criminal, if safety issues are involved in applying what is learned). In seminary classes, they are sinful. Teachers, we are warned in James 3:1, are to "receive greater judgment," so we need to do our absolute best in meriting the trust given to us by our institutions. Therefore, all factors involved in a successful classroom experience for students must be simultaneously put into play.

A successful teacher, we are continually told, moves from being teacher-centered to being student-centered, that is to say, from purely content-centered to learning-centered teaching. This is a challenge given the content-intensive nature of a discipline like theology. In the more liberal schools I attended, theology was considered a hands-on activity— "asking questions" being the definition of "doing theology." So, classes were discussion-driven. Usually, a fellow student would present a paper, or a professor would ask a question (e.g. "What is your God like?") and the rest was free-throw. (As one grad student instructor illustrated the issue to us: the question is whether the Gospel of Jesus Christ is an onion or an apple—whether truth is in the process as you peel it down or a central core at which you arrive.) In evangelical schools, given our belief that there is an actual *kerygma*, a *dogma*, a set of propositional truths that professors need to impart, classes have traditionally been lecture-driven. My classes are admittedly very lecture-heavy. I am not teaching a more hands-on kind of skill—like arithmetic, or even English literature, where reader response has become a key critical methodology. I'm teaching propositional truths. But, at the same time, these truths are revealed to be applied, so I do build in theological exercises and discussions that increase as the students master the basics and move to my more advanced courses. Class discussion activities are far greater in the advanced "Contemporary Theology and Theologians" class and my Master of Theology level course on Christology, than they are in Theology 1 and 2, but my task is not to be trendy. It is to make certain each student is moved a bit forward in knowledge from where she or he enters the course. The way to arrive at that goal varies as students acquire more information and more methodological skills. In a six-weeks course that process has to be streamlined, but it is always a process that needs to be monitored for success. The interaction with students in interviews centered around written assignments helps to keep in a hands-on component. And I always distribute my own (student signed) self-evaluation assessment wherein students report how much of the heavy reading list they have managed to read (for which they get extra credit if they read all assignments) and they can also tell me what illness or job or church or family trouble they had that impeded their work and thereby put in their plea for consideration. I also constructed my own several-page course evaluation sheets where (unsigned) they can critique the quality of books, lectures, the syllabus, the packet that accompanies the syllabus, the hand-outs, the Athanasian Scholars' performance, my own teaching, etc. These forms are for us, not for the school. Student generations change every three years these days, which is the length of our Master of Divinity

(MDiv) program (discounting those part-timers on what we call—hopefully hyperbolically—the "20-year plan"). Over the fifty years this year I've been teaching in educational institutions, thirty-nine of which have been teaching seminary, I've noticed that the general spirit of students shifts (e.g. sometimes toward the more conservative and conventional, sometimes toward the more justice-oriented and radical, sometimes missional, sometimes mega-church-oriented, sometimes para-church oriented, and on and on). While the kerygma's content doesn't change, the way of learning does.

For example, recently, one student told me he couldn't read hardcopy hand-outs, only e-copies sent to his computer. I send out electronic copies of the syllabus, but not every hand-out is in e-copy, especially the tried and true from years ago. So, I told him to scan it and he'd have his e-copy. He refused, whining, "But I want you to do it!" I was astonished. I explained I was inundated with grading re-doings and had no time to retype a hand-out he could scan himself. He didn't take any more courses with me, though he is cordial when we meet. To me, his is a new way to think I may have to consider accommodating in the future if it begins to replicate. I do put all class hand-outs in the hard-copy packet I distribute to accompany the syllabus on the first day. I also put some of these up on the documentary camera when I arrive at that point of the lecture where they are relevant, and, for outlines, I announce the page in the packet where they can be found. My Byington Scholar films every class and puts each on a protected site on YouTube open only to class student access, zooming in on the overheads (or adding stills of them in) and then emailing the links to the class so ELLs can watch them again and again to make sure they understand everything said in class and students who have to miss class can also keep up with class sessions.

But, in such a work-intensive course, I can't concede to every student request. One colleague whom I once invited to team-teach with me typed out every word of his lecture and distributed it in e-copy. I was impressed. But as many of my notes are hand-written, as are updatings typed, I have to pay for my own secretarial help. One has to decide where the finances one invests in the course will go, and I have decided to invest mine in Athanasian Scholars. As I explained to one student who complained the book list was too long, "I can't go home and read the required books to you. Just read what you can—you can work on the others for the rest of your life when you need them." There has to be a middle ground between professor and student. I set up the support and the opportunity to learn; they have to put in the effort.

Some students, of course, arrive already down the line of understanding the content of the discipline and move along toward expertise. Others enter at the beginning stage and gain ground. And some come from nowhere to expertise, given an agile mind and a hard work ethic. My goal each year is no dropouts. If we lose people for any other reasons than economic reversal, family catastrophes, ill health or, dropping dead—in other words, if they give up because they "just don't get it"—I consider this a failure on our part.

In my experience, the most truly successful learning is done by relationship. Most students want to succeed for teachers who obviously care about them and their progress and who have demonstrated that care by setting classes up in ways that encourage each student's success. It is also the way our God seems to disciple us.

DEPORTMENT IN THE INSTITUTION: POLITICS

One additional area to consider is Internecine Politics: stay out of them as much as possible.

Here is my simple personal view: the teacher's job is to make the administration look as good as possible, politically speaking. You want to help your bosses, deans, and department chairs run what appears to be a tight ship so that the president and the board of directors commend the administration. You are not there to give your bosses grief. That's not part of the job description. Freedom to run your class is not freedom to run off with it; it's a matter of trust that one is doing the job one is contracted to do, which is move one's students forward in the core curriculum one is supposed to be teaching. Contentious people who alienate students from administrators or spend their time politicking or complaining about their bosses and being uncooperative are let go and for good reasons. They should have studied Romans 13 and applied its teaching to their participation in Christian institutions. Of course, this assumes your boss is not taking credit for your work, stealing your ideas, making you do research outside your job description, hitting on you, holding you back so you can keep doing the good job you're doing while he or she slacks off, or all the other horrors attributed to (but not limited to) abuse in the secular system. If it happens, Romans 13 is not a pass card for abuse. But don't tackle it alone. Soak it in prayer and recruit trustworthy support.

The administrator's job is to make the task of teaching as pleasant and as supported as possible for the professors and to fight for their teachers and staff's increased benefits, wages, resources. A good administrator goes out of the way to make the teaching and administrative staff happy and secure and free to do the job as their expertise dictates it should be done, not overloading work or micromanaging classes, but concentrating on supplying needs and providing perks when merited. A slacking-off administrator, or one with a greed for power or on an ego trip, lording it over underlings, loses the best professors to other institutions, causes murmuring and votes of no confidence, and is eventually let go.

The body of Christ is intended to be symbiotic with Christ as boss and CEO and Chair of the Board. There is no power struggle about who is to be at the top. The answer in Christian institutions is Jesus. The rest of us are supposed to be fulfilling our job descriptions and, I believe, that begins with me doing my job most intentionally and faithfully to fulfill my calling and use my God-given abilities to the greatest extent that I can for the benefit of the students entrusted to me.

BRIEF HISTORY BEHIND THIS INSTRUCTIONAL METHODOLOGY

How did I come to develop this intentional instructional methodology? When I was young, I was in love with books and reading and kept mostly to myself. I would read and write for pleasure (a joy that has not altered with the years).

My mother, a child of the depression, foresaw me starving in an attic—the traditional image for writers—if I became a literature major, as I'd planned to be. So, she talked me into taking English Education in college and getting a certification as a fallback plan should I fail to write the great American novel. Thank God for mothers! They do know best. I've used that certificate at key moments and those skills ever since. Together, they are what qualified me to teach adult literacy in Louisville in the late 1970s and early 1980s.

When I became a Christian in 1966 and took to heart Jesus's "Great Commission" in Matthew 28:18-20, I went out on the city streets of the town where I was born with Moody Bible Institute Science tracts (because they were full of interesting information) to tell others about Jesus and his love.

When the riots swept across the urban United States, my same birth-town, Plainfield, New Jersey, also had a riot. Standing out on my parents' porch, listening to the shots in town, as the National Guard shot out the street lights, so the soldiers themselves wouldn't be well-lit targets, I sensed my call to urban ministry. It came amidst the realization that, as a child, I had walked and ridden my bike through all these streets and never sensed the estrangement there.

So, from 1966-1972, I was engaged in some aspect of urban ministry, mostly street work (in Plainfield, then Newark, then Philadelphia), in between studying, so the combination served as an action/reflection model for me. I am an intentional person and like to see each experience yielding as much benefit to all concerned as possible. I realize also I am product-oriented and measure the success of each experience by what it produces.

In 1969, my future wife and I had our first taste of inner city seminary education at the short-lived but wonderful Philadelphia expression of Gordon-Conwell Theological Seminary, the year Gordon Divinity School merged with Conwell School of Theology (which was the former Temple University School of Theology), thus becoming the Gordon-Conwell of today. Conwell had been offering a classic education enhanced by courses attuned to the needs of the urban world and this legacy has passed on to our Boston Campus. Given the urbanizing of the world's population, this legacy is addressing the nature and needs of the seminary of the future.

In 1970 (while I was completing my MDiv at Princeton Theological Seminary, where I'd transferred after the Philadelphia branch of GCTS closed), I interned as a college chaplain and developed that position into a half-time call for the next three and a half years. Among the speakers I invited was a city evangelist with whom I had done street work in Newark, New Jersey. When our chaplaincy ministry terminated in 1974, Bill Iverson invited my wife and me back to Newark to help him train seminarians in city ministry. He was working with New York Theological Seminary, then under Bill Webber (of *The Congregation in Mission* fame) and, as my wife and I were each completing Masters of Theology (ThM) degrees at that point, and, thus, were one degree advanced over those we supervised, we ended up teaching the basic Bible course for the seminary in New York and a variety of courses in Newark to the seminarians with whom we lived in a training community relationship. During this time, we spun off a parallel program for store front pastors (Alpha-Omega Community Theological School [ACTS]) who were attending our classes, but who were unable to enroll for lack of prior degrees past a high school diploma (and not all of them had completed that degree).

I found I could teach the store front pastors Greek, but not theology, since many could not read on a level advanced enough to handle theological discourse. But they were bright and could negotiate introductory Greek grammar. This was a great frustration to me, realizing I could not help students, despite their calling from God to learn, since they were not prepared to function at the reading level required to do introductory theological training.

I brought this burden with me when we went to Louisville so that my wife could pursue her doctorate in New Testament studies. If I could, I wanted to address this glaring gap in my education and teaching expertise and I did so by joining a fledgling literacy program.

After two years of running night classes in Laubach Literacy method, I became teaching coordinator for the Jefferson Country adult literacy program under Director Sharon Darling, being able now to take non-reading adults through literacy training into high school equivalency training. The second part of that process involved checking off check sheets detailing areas where students excelled, as well as where they needed to improve.

Adapting the concept to create a template for a cover sheet for term papers, when we arrived at Gordon-Conwell, my wife and I created a single checklist summary pages for each major assignment in all the classes we each taught and these have become the bases to guide our students as they master their written assignments (and theology course content), as well as the training tools from which we produce the grading guides our teaching colleagues use to correct assignments. The entire process is a way to help students negotiate the material and my Athanasian Teaching Scholars learn to master the art of teaching content in a manner that students can comprehend, thus helping each of them progress toward becoming future professors.

My wife and I also developed our own evaluation tools, a final self-evaluation set of pages for students to fill out, detailing the extent of their reading of required assignments, the nature of their work in the class, any impediments they encountered, and what they were able to take out of the classroom and apply to their ministries. A second set of course evaluation pages helps us evaluate the course and adjust assignment sheets, lectures, and class exercises to the altering nature of instruction required as times and technology change modes of thinking and the class cultural composition expands.

Thus, through the years, I have come to value a very intentional approach to teaching which strives to create a supportive environment that helps students maximize their ability to learn in both lectures and hands-on modes.

Appendix 1

Term Paper Assignment

Systematic Theology I

Required Assignment: Pick one attribute (characteristic) of God and show us how it helps us interpret an important issue in the church today.

Student Choices:

Select only one attribute of God you want to explore. To find an attribute, read "God's Self Revelation in Adjectives" in the packet, Chapter One, "The God of the Bible" in *The Global God*, and Part 3, "What is God Like?" in Erickson's *Christian Theology*. Select only one issue in the church to address. To find an issue, see suggestions on "The Sample Paper Topics" list at the end of this syllabus. Please note: if you want to choose a topic not on the list, you must ask the professor for approval.

Step One: Page One

Center Your Title on the First Page

By: (Put in Your Name)

Prof.

Class:

Campus:

Date:

Step Two: Pages Two and Three

- Write an introduction with a topical thesis and scope (two models are on the first page of the packet) briefly describing the attribute (that is to say, the characteristic) of God you will be helping your church to understand and the issue in the church to which you will be applying your understanding of that attribute as your interpretive tool (this is your topical thesis statement). Briefly show us the steps you will take to develop the connection between the attribute of God and the issue in the church (this is your scope). Make sure you have a strong topical thesis statement and scope (see examples on the first page of your packet).

- Do a word study of that attribute throughout the Bible.

- Use a concordance or a tool like *BibleWorks* to find references to your chosen attribute of God in the Old Testament. Look up each verse and read all the surrounding verses to see by its context what that word means. Make sure all verses are applying to God (not to people or any other reference).

- Please note: if there are many verses, select about one half dozen key representative ones.

- Write a declarative sentence stating simply what each Bible verse is saying, group these sentences into one paragraph summarizing your findings. These summary statements will be the OT biblical principles you will use as your interpretive tools.

- Next, use a concordance or a tool like *BibleWorks* to find the references to the attribute you are studying in the New Testament. Again, look up each verse and read all the surrounding verses to see by the context what that word means.

- Try to discuss at least one half dozen instances of the word to discover its various shades of meaning.

- Write a declarative sentence stating simply what each Bible verse is saying, group these sentences into one paragraph summarizing your findings. These will become the NT biblical principles you will use to interpret your issue.

- Finally, you may consult the meanings in the lexicons and consider what the information you have gleaned from your readings and the class lectures has to say about the attribute of God you have selected in order to supplement and refine your biblical summary statements.

- Now compare your list of OT and NT biblical principles to see which can be fused together and which add new dimensions to your understanding and should be listed separately. Can you draw out any additional conclusions to refine your interpretive biblical principles? Does the comparison add anything to your understanding of this characteristic of God?

- To end this section, double check to make certain you have summarized all your discoveries from your own word studies, supplemented by the lexicon definitions, assigned class readings and your wider reading, class lectures and discussions about your biblical findings to refine your interpretive principles (which you will very shortly be applying to the church issue you selected).

Step Three: Pages Four and Five

- Now introduce the current issue facing the Church which you selected. Show us why this issue is important. Consult various sources of information about this issue. Look at books, journals, surveys, Internet information (essays, websites, surveys, whatever is trustworthy and helpful), newspaper articles, news magazines, music lyrics, movies, interviews (or conduct interviews yourself), etc. Remember, all sources of information must be footnoted. Check with the librarian if you have questions about how a footnote should be written. Use *The Chicago Manual of Style*, Kate Turabian's *A Manual for Writers of Research Papers*, Nancy Vyhmeister's *Quality Research Papers*, or a similar style book. We are checking for consistency, whether you follow carefully whichever noting system you choose.

Step Four: Pages Six and Seven

- Apply your interpretive principles (the conclusion statements you made in part one that summarize what you learned about your chosen attribute of God) to the issue in the church you selected.

- In your analysis, make sure you are using the Bible verses and interpretive principles you drew up about the attribute of God you studied in part one and not drawing from new verses and using new attributes to interpret the issue (and make sure you stay focused on one issue). Remember, if you have not studied a particular verse or attribute of God in part one, do not introduce it and use it for your interpretive tool here in part two. Stick with the attribute and scriptural principles you studied in part one. Make sure the two halves of your paper interrelate. If you find you must add a new interpretive scripture verse in order to do your analysis of your issue, go back to your word study and replace a verse you have not used in your analysis with the new Bible verse. The corrected declarative sentence in your word study will now correspond to the new biblical interpretive principle you are now using in your analysis.

- After you have analyzed the issue, using your biblical principles as your interpreting tool, ask how you would help your church develop a position on this issue that is biblically sound (in other words, guided by the attribute of God with which you interpreted it).

- Draw out from your analysis practical ways in which Christians should act when confronting this issue. Summarize these into step by step recommendations for your parishioners to apply. Make sure these practical suggestions flow directly out of your analysis.

Step Five: Page Eight

- Now you are ready to draw your conclusion.

- Restate your thesis statement as a conclusion, tying together all your research. Provide a thought-provoking statement for people to ponder.

- BIBLIOGRAPHY and FOOTNOTES or ENDNOTES should be properly formatted. Remember to follow your selected style manual (e.g. *Chicago Manual of Style*, Turabian, Vyhmeister, Campbell/Ballou, Trimmer/McCrimmon, Modern Language Association, etc., whichever you chose) for proper format for your bibliography and your notes. Please notice, footnote and bibliographic entries are often not done in the same way, but will differ from each other. There is also a sample description in the packet and on the Library's Reserve shelves under "Research and Writing" you may consult. Ask the librarian for help if needed. Also, remember to double-space the text, using size 14 font and 1-inch margins, so we may write notes on content in the margins and make grammar corrections in the text. Don't forget to use the cover sheet to double-check your paper and make sure you have included all parts and aspects of the assignment (but don't fill it out—we'll do that for you). Attach the cover sheet to your draft and hand it in with your draft. Remember always to submit your previous draft and previous cover sheet with instructor's comments with each redoing. And never hesitate to consult the professor or Athanasian Teaching Scholars with your questions at the appropriate times and with the appropriate means suggested (telephone, email, texting, interviews) to help you complete the assignments. That is why we are here.

Appendix 2

Attach this cover sheet to your submission.

Name:

Telephone:

Email:

Paper: Theology I

Date:

From: William David Spencer

Grade:

The following items are rated according to the following symbols:

Y=yes

S=sometimes/somewhat

N=no

I=inadequate

A=adequate

G=good

S=superior

Methodology

Conclusions proved: I A G S

Exhaustive / comprehensive: I A G S

Accurate: I A G S

Insightful: I A G S

Original: I A G S

Sources are primary and creative: I A G S

Completeness of Study

Basis of Study is the Nature of God: N S Y

One attribute of God's character: N S Y

Word study of one attribute throughout the Bible: N S Y

Is your word study divided into OT and NT sections? N S Y

Did you study at least 6 passages from the OT? N S Y

Did you study at least 6 passages from the NT? N S Y

Are your own word study definitions presented before lexicon definitions? N S Y

Do you derive principles for interpretation from your study? N S Y

Did you use class textbooks? N S Y

Application to One Issue: N S Y

Did you tell us why this issue is crucial? N S Y

Is your issue well documented? N S Y

Did you interpret your issue using the principles derived from your Bible study? N S Y

Did you list practical suggestions for applying your findings to the church? N S Y

Did you draw out recommended actions directly from your analysis? N S Y

Did you include a bibliography and references? N S Y

Written Presentation

Well-Organized Paper (Both Halves of Your Paper Connect): N S Y

Introductory paragraph: N S Y

Topic stated: N S Y

Thesis stated: N S Y

Scope stated: N S Y

Body: N S Y

Summary: N S Y

Conclusion: N S Y

Literary style clear and succinct: N S Y

Spelling and grammar correct: N S Y

Do you need a remedial writing class? N S Y

Print easy to read? N S Y

Bibliography cited: N S Y

Facts and ideas of others noted in footnotes: N S Y

Footnotes & bibliography have a consistent and correct citation: N S Y

Comments:

c. 2017, William David Spencer

Chapter Ten

Language of the Seminary Classroom and the Language of the City

SEONG HYUN PARK

GORDON-CONWELL THEOLOGICAL SEMINARY'S VISION is *"To advance Christ's Kingdom in every sphere of life by equipping Church leaders to think theologically, engage globally, and live biblically."*[1]

At the Boston Campus of Gordon-Conwell, commonly known as the Center for Urban Ministerial Education (CUME), the phrase "engage globally" takes a more concrete scope: engage Boston and beyond.

The key Scripture that has shaped CUME's educational mission in the inner-city of Boston comes from Jeremiah 29:7: "Seek the welfare of the city where I have sent you into exile, and pray to the Lord on its behalf, for in its welfare you will find your welfare." (NRSV)

In the words of Eldin Villafañe, the founding director of CUME, this verse represents a paradigm that stems from "a theology of context, a theology of mission, and a theology of spirituality"[2] effectively captured in three keywords of *presence, peace,* and *prayer*: a *presence* that calls for *"critical engagement"* (rather than "assimilation," "revolution," or "escapism"); *peace* (*shalom*) that speaks of "wholeness, soundness, completeness, health, harmony, reconciliation, justice, welfare—both personal and social;" and

---

1. Gordon-Conwell's Vision, Mission and Purpose.
2. Eldin. *Seek the Peace of the City: Reflections on Urban Ministry,* 1–3.

prayer—or spirituality—"needed to struggle and live in the city."[3] In short, seeking the formation of the people of God who will live out such presence, *shalom* and prayerful life in the city is the mission of CUME.

HISTORY OF BOSTON

Who are these "people" of God that CUME trains to live out the paradigm of Jeremiah 29:7? In today's Boston, a large proportion of these "people" are the immigrant population that have arrived in the city following the 1965 Act, and, therefore, many are English Language Learners (ELL). If these newcomers are to critically engage in the life of the city; to actively seek the "wholeness, soundness, completeness, health, harmony, reconciliation, justice, welfare" of Boston, and to heartily bear the "struggle" of the life of the city in their prayers, then their ability to effectively communicate in the language of the city, i.e., English, is a necessary condition.

WHAT HAPPENED IN LATE 1960s?

In 1968, the American immigration policy shifted from one based on national origin to one based on skilled labor, prioritizing the reunion of the immigrant families. This enactment of the Immigration and Naturalization Act of 1965 greatly altered the demographic mix of the immigrants entering America, and along with many other cities, Boston became the destination of many immigrants from Asia, Africa, and Latin America. To illustrate the point, the population of the native-born in Boston has remained fairly constant between 1980 (475,938) and 2015 (479,346), an increase of a mere 0.7 percent. During the same period, the population of the foreign—born in Boston has increased from 87,056 in 1980 to 190,123 in 2015, an increase of 218.4 percent, and most of these originate from countries where English is not the primary language.[4]

---

3. Ibid.
4. Ciurczak, "Boston's Foreign Born Population, A Breakdown."

IMMIGRANTS AND THE CHANGING CHURCH DEMOGRAPHICS

One significant impact that this influx of immigrants has had in the Christian community of Boston is that the new church plants since the late 1960s would largely be done for these new immigrant communities. Based on the research conducted by the Emmanuel Gospel Center (EGC), there were 300 Christian churches in the city of Boston in 1969. This number grew to 459 by 1993, and to 575 by 2010.[5] What is remarkable is that the growth observed during these decades was one that overcame a continuing decline in the mainline Protestant churches and Roman Catholic churches over the same period—a growth happening "in non-mainline systems, non-English speaking systems, denominations you have never heard of, churches that meet in storefronts, churches that meet on Sunday afternoons."[6]

To clarify, churches that are primarily Anglo or Anglo/multiethnic did see growth too. For instance, the Anglo churches accounted for 14 of the 100 newly planted churches between 2000-2005. Of the 86 remaining new churches, however, 43 were Hispanic, Haitian, Brazilian, Asian, and African, and the rest Caribbean, African-American and of other ethnic groups.[7]

The main factor contributing to this "Quiet Revival" in Boston, as Doug Hall of EGC calls it, is the presence of the new immigrant groups that arrived following the enactment of the 1965 Act who were largely non-European in origin and non-native speakers of English. The post-1965 Act worship landscape of Boston suddenly filled with many tongues from around the globe, each attended and pastored by the speakers of that particular language.

NON-ENGLISH SEMINARY CLASSES AT CUME, 1976-2016

It is no surprise, then, that CUME—the Boston Campus of Gordon-Conwell Theological Seminary– would be responding to the needs of the time by offering seminary classes in languages such as Spanish, Portuguese, and Haitian Creole, in addition to English. Right from the beginning, in other words, 1976, CUME has made the best of its efforts to offer classes in both English and Spanish. In fact, CUME kept publishing its English-Spanish

5. Daman, "Understanding Boston's Quiet Revival," lines 33–64.

6. Daman, "EGC's Research Uncovers the Quiet Revival," 2.

7. Daman, "Understanding Boston's Quiet Revival."

bilingual course catalog all the way through the 1980s when immigrants from Brazil entered the scene and CUME started adding Portuguese into the mix, as well as Haitian Creole, and even Khmer to a certain degree.

As a seminary campus, CUME's mission is to serve the churches,[8] and one of the areas where the churches' needs were most direly felt during the period of CUME's first forty years of ministry in the city (1976-2016) has been in the theological education of the pastors and leaders of the churches where the ministry for the local congregants had to be carried out in the language of their country of origin.

Against this backdrop, the contribution of CUME in the life of the churches in Boston needs to be assessed. The revival that has sustained itself for over four decades in the city of Boston, a revival that has quietly filled the ministry needs of the growing immigrant churches in the city, would not have been witnessed without the presence of the pastors and leaders of the immigrant churches whom CUME has trained in the languages they and their congregants read the Bible, worship, and communicate.

LANGUAGES OF INSTRUCTION AT GCTS–BOSTON, 2017 AND ONWARD

After 40 years of ministry in educating pastors and leaders in the city, the Boston Campus of Gordon-Conwell continues to be committed to making theological education accessible in English and in the major languages of the immigrant churches in the city.

What is new in 2017 and onward is the listing of acquisition of competency in English as a learning outcome in the classes taught in a language other than English. As noted earlier, CUME is a seminary campus in Boston that seeks the formation of the people of God who in turn will seek the *presence* that calls for "critical engagement," the *peace* (shalom) that speaks of "wholeness, soundness, completeness, health, harmony, reconciliation, justice, welfare—both personal and social," and the *prayer* needed to "struggle and live in the city."

Such an engagement in the life of the city would simply not be possible without communicating with the city, in the language of the city—English.

For the sake of clarity, this is not to suggest that English is the "right" language either for the theological education of the pastors or the worship experience of their congregants in the immigrant church context. On the

8. Gordon-Conwell Theological Seminar, "Mission and Purpose."

contrary, an effective education of the minister will certainly require the delivery of the curricular content in the language in which the learner is most fluent. It is the conviction of CUME, however, that the fulfillment of their ministry efforts must result in bearing fruits of "wholeness, soundness, completeness, health, harmony, reconciliation, justice, welfare" in the city in which they minister.

In practical terms, this means that the instructors who teach at CUME in languages other than English will design the instruction with strategies built into the curriculum that foster the acquisition of competence in English, with the Jeremiah Paradigm for the City in view (i.e., Jeremiah 29:7).[9] The strategy can be as simple as assigning a portion of the required reading to be done in English. A curricular model with which we are experimenting in fall 2017 is to structure the Critical Thinking and Writing course to intersect with the Old Testament Survey course in Spanish where one of the assignments in one course will be examined in the other and reading and writing in English will be encouraged.

Theological education at the Boston Campus of Gordon-Conwell is not complete without the graduates and their congregations seeking to be present in the city through critical engagement, causing *shalom* in every aspect of the life of the city, while praying for the city. Such an engagement cannot become a practice without communicating in the language of the city, and, thus, competence in the language of the city—English, in Boston's case—becomes a critical learning outcome in all the courses taught in languages other than English at CUME.

9. Villafañe.

Conclusion

Aída Besançon Spencer

I WAS BORN AN English Language Learner and an immigrant in a strange land. I was born in the Dominican Republic, my mother was from Puerto Rico, my father from the Netherlands. At first I was taught three languages (Spanish, Dutch, and English) until I became so garbled that I spoke no language at all. My parents brought me to a psychiatrist who, upon hearing of my former trilingual state, told my parents to begin with one language. That language was Spanish. But when I went to school, to "Fun-to-learn" (the school's euphemism for "kindergarten"), I was taught in English. At home, my father spoke to me in English while my mother spoke to me in Spanish. (Dutch was dropped by the wayside.) At first English was my second language, but, now, after many years in the United States, English has become my primary language.

In the Dominican Republic, I was registered as a Dominican at first, then I was later also registered as a United States citizen born abroad. I thus became an immigrant in the land of my birth and an immigrant in the land of my dwelling (when we moved to the U.S. just before I entered sixth grade at ten years of age). Therefore, I can identify with both the English Language Learner and the English Language Teacher! I am forever the stranger who travels with the Strange God, Creator of the Universe, who, although having created and is now sustaining earth, when on earth had no place to call home (Luke 9:58).[1]

Because I am bilingual, many U.S. employers appreciate my facility in Spanish. I worked with Latin Americans in New Jersey as a community

---

1. See further A. Spencer 1998:89-105.

143

organizer, taught English as a Second Language (ESL) in adult education, and even in a maximum security prison. I began a doctorate in ESL but settled on New Testament studies. I am not the only contributor to this volume who was born and reared in a multilingual and multinational situation. So were Olga Soler and Seong Hyun Park. We have needed help from others and, after receiving such help, were able to give help to others. Thus, reading *Empowering English Language Learners* has been particularly interesting to me.

SUMMARY

What have I learned from this volume? I have learned that "immigrant" is a broad category. We might even say that the first immigrants were Adam and Eve when they were ushered out of Paradise into a fallen world. Yet even in this fallen world, they were clothed by the Creator they had just disobeyed (Gen. 3:21, 23). God is compassionate and just. God's impact on these immigrants—humans— has continued through all these thousands of years. Several biblical concepts have been repeatedly mentioned as crucial in this book, such as hospitality to the stranger, loving this new neighbor who is also created in God's image, the three dimensional Trinity, the Beloved Community who creates community, and teaching ELLs as a ministry that serves the Lord.

Many strategies for successfully empowering ELLs have been made by experienced and effective teachers and administrators in secular and Christian settings to students of all age levels. The importance of these strategies has been indicated by their repetition. Respect for the student and the teacher is crucial. After all, ELLs are pacesetters. Eye contact is indispensable. Creativity in instruction, including using the arts, is also important for, after all, our God is the Creator. A supportive community encourages education and mutual love and relationship-building. Prayer for wisdom, success, and protection is key to the all-powerful and loving God. A love for learning can infuse the student if it is felt by the teacher. Love includes learning about this new neighbor's culture. Sharing stories can be helpful. Hope and encouragement need to be given because our God is a God of hope and encouragement. Humility is always necessary, even to the extent of allowing students to teach teachers when appropriate. When teaching those for whom English is not the primary language, repeating the basics is crucial, which includes pre-teaching, explaining, and defining vocabulary.

Small groups allow students to learn better and to express themselves more regularly. Allowing students to re-do written assignments reduces their anxiety and furthers their education. All the teachers in this volume are student-oriented in that their goal is for all students to learn and teachers' teaching is focused on that overall goal. Excellent teaching must be intentional. It affects the teachers' style, content, and methodology. However, the teacher must also have self-care, provide a structure that is both flexible and firm, modeling what he or she teaches. And, throughout, gentle humor may help in an anxious situation, even as Jesus called James and John "Sons of Thunder" when they erroneously called for the destruction of their non-believing Samaritan neighbors (Luke 9:52-22; Mark 3:17).

FINAL THOUGHTS

Even though I now teach in English to adults desiring to serve God in present and future ministries, I have, especially in recent years, attracted many international students to my New Testament classes. I have tried to apply many of the strategies mentioned: respect for students, encouragement, clarification, no belittling or making fun of mistakes, compassionate concern, reduction of anxiety, dialogue, and humility. In one class I had about seventy-five percent Asians (in a school where Asians were about ten percent). The few Anglo-Americans I also had initially looked lost! My husband, upon visiting, said it looked like an Asian summit! (Usually about half of my class has international students.) I think the ELLs could sense that I welcomed them and treated them as a normal part of the educational life. Of course, we humans are multinational and multiracial. God created us this way and to such a world we are going, a world inhabited by "all tribes and peoples and languages" who agree that salvation belongs to the one God seated on the throne (Rev. 7:9-10). In the meantime, I have made so many blunders upon pronouncing names! I take attendance regularly so that I can eventually remember the students' names. But they are patient and understanding. Lately, I have added more small group discussions to encourage individual participation. Instead of asking a series of questions on the readings to the whole class, I have broken the class into several small groups where different questions are answered in the different small groups and then one student from each group reports back to the whole class. It takes more time, but the students are happier and the answers are much more thorough.

I have always been attentive to simplifying my own vocabulary and thinking about what vocabulary might not be recognized. But I cannot always perceive which words will be unknown to the listeners, so I may ask if they know what a certain word means, because adult students accomplished in their own spheres may be too embarrassed to ask publically. For example, the other day I returned from a conference with left-over free subway tickets for use in Boston. So, I asked my students in a class if anyone could use these tickets. No one raised their hands, but after class an international student came up and said his family members who were visiting could use the tickets. Consequently, I asked, "Are you going to Boston?" He answered, "My extended family plans on eating." I was baffled. Why would they go to Boston to eat when they could eat nearby? Then it came to me. For me, "subway" meant Metro transportation. For him, "subway" meant Subway fast food sandwiches. That took a while to figure out. My tickets would do him no good.

As does my husband, the Rev. Dr. William David Spencer, my allowing students to re-do papers during the semester is a great help to all but especially to ELLs. One student spent two hours trying to understand my script notes on his papers. My teaching assistant was able to read them and explain them to him in only fifteen minutes. As a result, his grade improved one grade level. Students who travel many hours and miles to learn across borders and languages want to learn and want to succeed in their new country in an institution with new ways of learning. Their parents and churches may be subsidizing their education and, thus, the students want to please them. Miscommunication among those of the same language can frequently occur, but how much more happens across different languages and cultures? Allowing re-doings helps so much and, as well, reduces student complaints.

In the past, I taught English as the content in ESL classes. Now, in graduate school, I teach the New Testament as the content, but English is the means to learn that content. Some aspects of teaching ESL are applicable to all ELLs. One summer many years ago, I taught several classes in one room at the same time, using programed learners (ESL and GED high school equivalency). It was havoc, running back and forth answering all sorts of different questions and then lecturing at different times for parts of the class. I was at my maximum level of concentration. I had to become flexible. That same flexibility is helpful now with ELLs seeking to learn the New Testament as they plan to please God in ministry. And I try to be attentive to facial signs indicating students want to speak up. When I taught ESL to Spanish-speaking inmates in a prison, I had to treat them as fellow human beings, not "criminals" different from me, because I reminded myself, if we are honest, we know that we are all criminals in some way, but all our crimes are not ones against the State. In a similar manner, ELLs are fellow human beings in a situation much like mine whenever I travel to another country. In the prison, I tried to be welcoming to the students, but yet, as a woman in an all-male environment, I had to be wise. I wore more conservative clothing than normal. I was careful I did not get caught in any practice to undermine the safety of the prison (by, for example, mailing inmates' letters not being sent through the system). Now, too, I am conscious of appropriate attire. My God is a God of truth as well as love. I must keep watch over the borders I set to maintain my integrity. The inmates were mostly very respectful, but every once in a while a student would ask a question that was on the edge of disrespectfulness or on the edge of my knowledge. I always take seriously all questions and do not respond in kind but try to "keep my cool." After all, I can be confident because God as the God of truth has the answer. Jesus himself answered many antagonistic questions while on earth. He psyched out the questioner's intentions. For example, instead of directly answering the antagonistic question by some religious rulers, "By what authority are you doing these things?" he asked them his own question, "Did the baptism of John come from heaven, or was it of human origin?" (Luke 20:1-4 NRSV). As a result, they were stymied. Of course, I cannot perceive peoples' genuine thoughts behind their questions as Jesus did, but I can rely on God to help me. So I try to listen carefully. I try to be clear, but, from time to time, I may have to diffuse antagonism with confidence and firmness, while maintaining mutual respect.

In summary, empowering ELLs is a very important topic for all teachers. This book has provided strategies for success from Christian educators that rest on training and experience and on the leading of the God revealed in the Bible who is "Lord God, compassionate and merciful, slow to be displeased and greatly loving and faithful" (Exod. 34:6). This mighty God loves every stranger, is not partial but rather executes justice for all (Deut. 10:17-18).[2] And this is the Guide all teachers should try to emulate.

2. See further Spencer 1998:30-34, 97.

About the Authors

DEAN BORGMAN holds a BA (Wheaton College), MA (Fairfield University, Columbia University) and a Certificate of Advanced Graduate Standing (Northeastern University). He founded and directs the Center for Youth Studies, a national and global network of those interested in research about adolescence and the youth culture. His areas of expertise include urban and cross-cultural youth ministry and the changing youth culture. He taught history and social sciences at New Canaan High School and New York City Community College. In addition to teaching history, he was chairman of the social sciences division at Cuttington College in Liberia, Africa. He also served as educational director of street academies for the New York Urban League.

Professor Borgman is a leader in youth ministries. He established Young Life in New England and founded their Urban Training Institute. For eight summers, he directed and spoke at two of Young Life's camps. He also worked to integrate young people's involvement in Young Life and St. Christopher's Episcopal Chapel. He has served on the Youth Board of the Episcopal Diocese of New York and the Youth, Urban and Spiritual Renewal Commissions of the Episcopal Diocese of Massachusetts.

Professor Borgman wrote "A History of American Youth Ministry" for Benson and Senter's *The Complete Book of Youth Ministries* (1987). Since 1985, he has been writing for the *Encyclopedia of Youth Studies* (www.centerforyouth.org). His chapter, "Bridging the Gap: From Social Science to Congregations, Researchers to Practitioners," appears in Eugene Roehlkepartain, et al.'s *The Handbook of Spiritual Development in Childhood and Adolescence* (2006).

Professor Borgman is an Episcopal priest and was invited by Archbishop George Carey to be youth ministry consultant to the 1998 Lambeth Conference. He and his wife, Gail, have four children: John, Deborah,

Matthew and Christen, eleven grandchildren, and reside in Rockport, Massachusetts.

His publications include: *Hear My Story: Understanding the Cries of Troubled Youth* (Hendrickson Publishers, 2003), *God at the Mall: Youth Ministry That Meets Kids Where They're At* (Hendrickson Publishers, 1999), *Agenda for Youth Ministry* (with C. Cooke, SPCK Publishing, 1998), *When Kumbaya Is Not Enough: A Practical Theology for Youth Ministry* (Hendrickson Publishers, 1997).

His areas of expertise include: Culture/Youth, Youth Ministries, Urban Development, Postmodernism, Racial Reconciliation, Justice, Episcopal Church.

JENNIFER CREAMER holds a BA (University of the Pacific), two MA degrees (Gordon-Conwell Theological Seminary), and a PhD (North-West University, South Africa). Her dissertation, *God as Creator in Acts 17:24: An Historical-Exegetical Study* was recently published by the Africanus Monograph Series of Wipf and Stock Publishing. Since 2014, Jennifer is an adjunct professor (GCTS Boston) of New Testament Survey and Basic Greek. For more than twenty years, she has taught biblical studies at the University of the Nations in various international locations. Jennifer is a member of the editorial team of the *Africanus Journal*. She is ordained in the Cumberland Presbyterian Church and serves as Pastor of Organization at Pilgrim Church (Beverly, Massachusetts). Her publications include articles, such as "Who is Theophilus? Discovering the Original Reader of Luke–Acts," *In Die Skriflig* 48, no. 1 (June 2014): Art. #1701 and "Making Known the Unknown God: An Exploration of Greco-Roman Backgrounds Related to Paul's Areopagus Speech," *Africanus Journal* 3, no. 2 (November 2011): 43–55.

JULIA BUTLER DAVIS holds a BS in Education from Wilberforce University, an ED.M from the Harvard Graduate School of Education, and an ED.M from Bouve College of Health Sciences at Northeastern University. She has held teaching certificates in New York, Massachusetts, and the District of Columbia and has been certified as an Assistant Principal and as an Assistant Special Education Supervisor. Julia has taught in the public and private sector in community-based programs including METCO, Summer STEP opportunities for underrepresented populations in science and technology and Head Start. She has served as a member of the Parent Advocacy Group for Massachusetts supporting FAPE and mainstreaming Special Education students. She has taught pre-K through all 12 grades, Adult Non- Readers, Limited English Language Learner's and GED Preparation courses. Julia taught internationally as an undergraduate exchange student in a Special Education Program based in Chepstow, Wales, which operated under the auspices of Antioch College in Ohio.

Julia and her husband Dan have three children and three grandchildren. They attend the International Family Church in North Reading, Massachusetts. Julia developed a weekly prayer breakfast program for the Cambridge, MA community.

Click this link to view Julia at the CUME GCTS Chapel in Boston outlining strategies for empowering Special Education Students https://www.youtube.com/watch?v=WKRN_XAvwHU&t=1s. Contact Julia at 781-393-4517 for speaking engagements.

JEANNE DEFAZIO is a SAG/AFTRA actress of Spanish/ Italian descent, who played supporting parts in theater, movies, and television series before disappearing into a life of service to the marginalized in the drama of real life. Jeanne became a teacher of second-language-learning children in the barrios of San Diego. A woman of great faith, intelligence, and energy, she completed a Bachelor of Arts in History at the University of California, Davis, pursued seminary education at Gordon-Conwell Theological Seminary (MAR Theology), and completing a Cal State Teach English Language Learners Program. From 2009 to the present, Jeanne has returned as an Athanasian Teaching Scholar at Gordon Conwell's multicultural Boston Campus Center for Urban Ministerial Education (CUME), which serves the often unnoticed but thriving ethnic churches. Jeanne has co-authored with Teresa Flowers: *How to Have an Attitude of Gratitude on the Night Shift*, edited *Creative Ways to Build Christian Community* (with John P. Lathrop), *Redeeming the Screens*, (with William David Spencer) and *Berkeley Street Theatre*.

Resources

View LeaAnn Pendergrass's Uniting the Nations interview with Jeanne DeFazio: https://www.youtube.com/watch?v=nSFMoAJuPRk and Gemma Wenger's interview of Jeanne DeFazio, Charlie Lehman, and Jozy Pollock regarding *Berkeley Street Theatre*: https://youtu.be/kP5ntLpdurM. Email Jeanne at jcdefazio55@gmail.com. She will be happy to speak at events.

JAN DEMPSEY received her BA from Gordon College and her MLIS from the University of Rhode Island. She is currently the Library Director at the

Hamilton-Wenham Public Library in Hamilton, Massachusetts. She also oversees the church library at the First Congregational Church in Revere, MA. She enjoys beekeeping, gardening, and grandchildren.

MICHAEL DEMPSEY graduated from Gordon College with a degree in Chemistry and worked as a Research Scientist for several years. He worked with computers and eventually started his own computer networking company. In 2010, he sold his company and retired in 2013. Since then he has been an enthusiastic volunteer and Director of the ESL Program at First Congregational Church in Revere, MA. He also volunteers on several town boards in Groveland, MA for the Conservation Commission, Community Preservation Committee, and directs a town event facility at Veasey Memorial Park. He is passionate about immigration and the environment, and is also active on his church's Building and Finance Board.

JEAN DIMOCK received her MA and DMin. degrees from Gordon-Conwell Theological Seminary at its Boston Center for Urban Ministerial Education (CUME). Her doctoral research and thesis concerned domestic violence. She is now a domestic violence specialist who served as a New Hampshire guardian *ad litem* and works with women across the nation who find themselves in domestic violence homes. She helps the children in these situations by giving the adults understanding as to what their children are experiencing. Jean is also an adjunct professor teaching philosophy, ethics, and various psychology courses within the State University system of New Hampshire at Great Bay Community College in Portsmouth. She lives on the New Hampshire Seacoast and has two children, two grandchildren, two felines, and one husband.

SEONG HYUN PARK, MA, PhD is the Dean of Boston Campus, the Director of Research and Publications, and Assistant Professor of Old Testament, at GCTS. Dr. Park joined Gordon-Conwell in 2004 after years of extensive archaeological work in Israel, and teaching internationally in Argentina and Palestine. Fluent in four languages—Korean, Spanish, English and Modern Hebrew—he currently teaches Old Testament and Biblical Archaeology. His archaeological fieldwork included surveying Middle Bronze sites in the Jordan Valley and an Iron Age Judahite tomb in Jerusalem, and supervising field excavations of the Persian stratum in the Philistine port-city of Ashkelon, Hellenistic-Roman tombs in the Valley of Hinnom in Jerusalem, and the Iron Age palace of King Ahab in Tel Jezreel. He has published numerous articles about his fieldwork and other subjects related to Israel and the Old Testament.

Dr. Park was also the acting director of Harvard University's Ashkelon Archaeological Laboratory in Israel, and was a conference session chair at the 5th World Archaeological Congress in Washington, D.C.

He previously taught at Bethlehem Bible College in Bethlehem, Palestine, and in Seminario Teológico Tirano in Buenos Aires, Argentina.

He is co-editor of the *Africanus Journal* and the Africanus Monograph Series, and recently co-edited *Reaching for the New Jerusalem: A Biblical and Theological Framework for the City* (Wipf & Stock, 2013), a volume in the Urban Voice Series for which he serves as the series editor. Dr. Park's scholarly interests include the Old Testament and its cultures, Biblical Hebrew, the analysis of cities in Iron Age Israel, and interpreting the Bible in the context of its own land. His personal interests include music, photography and travel. Dr. Park proposed to his wife, Dr. Hyun Gyung Jang, in the Garden of Gethsemane, Jerusalem.

OLGA SOLER is director/writer and performer for Estuary Ministries, a Christ-centered performing arts ministry dealing with biblical themes, inner healing, abuse, and addictive problems. The art forms used include drama, dance, storytelling, mime, comedy, graphic arts, writing, film, and song. Olga attended the High School of Performing Arts ("Fame"), the Lee Strasberg Theater Institute, and the Herbert Berghof Studios in New York City. She has performed widely at conferences, churches, prisons, coffee houses, support groups, youth groups, and retreats and has even performed on the streets at secular colleges, and in worship services across the United States and the United Kingdom. She holds degrees in education and communications with equivalent studies in theology and psychology. She studied for two years at Gordon-Conwell Theological Seminary. She has designed and conducted the workshops "Dance Alive" and "Trauma Drama" at many Christian Recovery conferences. She wrote the curriculum for and conducted Discovery Groups for addicts at the Boston Rescue Mission, using the arts to help them process aspects of their recovery. She also conducts workshops for Christian drama and dance in many churches of all denominations. Using Paulo Freire's "pedagogy of the oppressed," she wrote a script for the "Mosaics" group of parents helping their children who were victims of sexual abuse through the courts system and assisted them in filming the script for a documentary. She performed and coauthored scripts for four years with the "Team" Christian Ministry in

Massachusetts and conducted eight full-scale multimedia presentations out of the Rio Ondo Arts Place in Woburn, MA, including "Voice of the Martyrs," "Techno Easter," and "Clean Comedy Night." She has directed and choreographed entire productions at universities and colleges, including "A Man for All Seasons," "Jane Eyre," "Amahl and the Night Visitors," and (by permission of the author) Calvin Miller's "The Singer." She wrote and illustrated the book *Epistle to the Magadalenes* and has conducted retreats for women using the book accompanied by dramatic presentation. She is the author of many other books and assorted screenplays. She is the proud mother of three wonderful children: Cielo, Reva, and Ransom. She lives in Massachusetts with her husband Chris and her Japanese Chin (dog), Kiji.

Olga sends this message to readers: "If you have any questions about what you read in my chapter, or if you would like to hear, as Paul Harvey used to say, 'the rest of the story,' I am available to you. I speak publicly about intentional community, healing, support, and recovery (from abuse and addiction), domestic violence, the media (the blessings and the curses of), and the arts from a biblical perspective. I punctuate all my talks with what I have just mentioned, demonstrating how these are used well and advocating for their use in worship, teaching, and evangelism. I do workshops on dance (Davidic and liturgical), drama, storytelling, mime, and the arts as a healing or community-building medium. I also speak to school and home-school groups about alternative methods for help with dyslexia, ADD, and ADHD. I have traveled all over the United States and the United Kingdom speaking, and am available for a small stipend, travel, and board expenses. If anyone in your congregation does not mind a house guest for an evening, I am happy to fellowship with my brothers and sisters anywhere. I also have many books available, which I can send you in e-book format for a donation. These include: *The Body* (illustrated, book about the church from Genesis to Revelation); *Primer for Home Fellowship*; *Tough Inspiration from the Weeping Prophet* (about domestic violence); *Who Am I?* (about children); *Epistle to the Magdalenes* (illustrated); and *Adoni*, the psalms of a woman (illustrated book of deep spiritual poetry). I have collaborated on other books: *Just Don't Marry One*, edited by Yancy and Yancy, and *Creative Ways to Build Christian Community*, edited by Jeanne DeFazio and John Lathrop, *Redeeming the Screens* (ed. by Jeanne DeFazio and William David Spencer), and *Berkeley Street Theatre* (ed. Jeanne DeFazio). Contact me by email at fleursavag@aol.com.

AIDA BESANÇON SPENCER holds a BA (Douglass College, Rutgers University), MDiv, ThM (Princeton Theological Seminary), and PhD (Southern Baptist Theological Seminary). She is Senior Professor of New Testament at Gordon-Conwell Theological Seminary. Born and reared in Santo Domingo, Dominican Republic, she has taught in the Caribbean and in Spanish on various occasions. Dr. Spencer has worked as a community organizer, social worker, minister, and educator in a wide variety of urban settings. She has taught English as a Second Language at several adult centers, organized Christian outreach at Trenton State Prison, and served as the campus chaplain of the College of New Jersey (formerly Trenton State College).

Her publications include *The Goddess Revival* (first printed with Baker 1995 and then reprinted by Wipf and Stock), *Beyond the Curse: Women Called to Ministry* (Baker, 1985), *Second Corinthians: Bible Study Commentary* (with W. D. Spencer, Zondervan, 1989), *The Prayer Life of Jesus: Shout of Agony, Revelation of Love, a Commentary* (with W. D. Spencer, University Press of America, 1990), *Joy Through the Night: Biblical Resources on Suffering* (with W. D. Spencer, InterVarsity, 1994, reprinted by Wipf and Stock), *Latino Heritage Bible* (co-edited with others, World Bible, 1995), *Paul's Literary Style: A Stylistic Comparison of II Corinthians 11:16-12:13, Romans 8:9-39, and Philippians 3:2-4:13* (University Press of America, 1998), *God through the Looking Glass: Glimpses from the Arts* (co-editor W. D. Spencer, Baker, 1998), *The Global God: Multicultural Evangelical Views of God* (co-editor W. D. Spencer, Baker, 1998), *Second Corinthians: Daily Bible Commentary* (Hendrickson, 2007), *Global Voices on Biblical Equality: Women and Men Ministering Together in the Church* (co-editors W. D. Spencer and M. Haddad, Wipf and Stock, 2008), *Marriage at the Crossroads: Couples in Conversation About Discipleship, Gender Roles, Decision Making and Intimacy* (co-authors: W. D. Spencer, S. Tracy and C. Tracy, InterVarsity, 2009), *1 Timothy*, New Covenant Commentary Series (Cascade, 2013), *Titus, 2 Timothy*, New Covenant Commentary Series (Cascade, 2014), *Reaching for the New Jerusalem* (co-editors S. H. Park and W. D. Spencer, Wipf and Stock, 2013), and almost 200 chapters, articles, and reviews.

An ordained minister in the Presbyterian Church (USA), Rev. Spencer is the founding pastor of organization of the Pilgrim Church of Beverly. She has been a visiting scholar at Harvard Divinity School and El Seminario Evangélico of Puerto Rico.

She is listed in *Who's Who in Religion, Contemporary Authors, Who's Who of American Women, Who's Who in America, Who's Who in the World,*

Who's Who in American Education and *Who's Who among American Teachers and Educators*. Her scholarly interests include Paul's letters, Luke and Acts, the New Testament and women, New Testament ministry, and the New Testament and literary style and imagery. Her personal interests include reading fiction, walking, and gardening. She and her husband William live in Hamilton, MA.

WILLIAM DAVID SPENCER is Distinguished Adjunct Professor of Theology and the Arts at Gordon-Conwell Theological Seminary's Boston Campus/ Center for Urban Ministerial Education (CUME). He has been teaching formally in a variety of educational institutions since 1968. He won the Nancy Higginson Dore Prize for excellence in education at Rutgers University, where he earned his bachelors in English Education, certifying him as a secondary education English teacher. He became serious about his faith in Jesus Christ at the Rutgers/Douglass InterVarsity Christian Fellowship. In college, he did his first street evangelism and with friends started an evangelistic band, the Spheres, performing across the eastern seaboard. After a year studying at the former Philadelphia center of Gordon-Conwell, he earned a Master of Divinity degree, with a New Testament concentration in the Greek and Hebrew track, at Princeton Theological Seminary. He also did city ministry in Newark (NJ) with Crosscounter, Inc. and in west Philadelphia with Ethos and the Presbytery of Philadelphia, setting up block associations to bring racial reconciliation and helping set up and run two evangelistic coffeehouses. At the same time, he co-led an evangelistic gospel band sponsored by the ministry of opera singer Jerome Hines.

After graduating, he became Protestant Chaplain at Rider College (now University) and was ordained as a Presbyterian minister. He also volunteered at a ministry his wife began in Trenton State Prison with Hispanic inmates. As he and his wife were completing their Master of Theology (THM) degrees in Christian Higher Education, also at Princeton Theological Seminary, they were called back to Newark to teach basic Bible interpretation and supervise seminarians in urban ministry for a joint program of New York Theological Seminary, Crosscounter, Inc., and The Salvation Army Newark Central Corps. In addition, they created the college level Alpha-Omega Community Theological School (ACTS) for storefront pastors who were attending their courses, expanding to four centers: two in Newark, one in Jersey City (NJ), and another in the Bedford Stuyvesant area of Brooklyn, working with The Salvation Army, the Church of God in Christ (COGIC), and The King's College. The program had 100 students and 15 professors. After that entire ministry closed, he accompanied his wife to Louisville, Kentucky, so she could earn her doctorate. He became a Laubach literacy teacher in a pioneering adult literacy program with the Jefferson County, Kentucky, Board of Education. After two years, he became teaching coordinator for the county, where he established and supervised eight literacy and GED centers in the city of Louisville and surrounding towns. He also authored a pamphlet on how to begin a literacy center and co-authored a reading materials assessment booklet, both published by the Jefferson County Board of Education Adult Program. After his wife's graduation and invitation to teach at Gordon-Conwell Theological Seminary, he accompanied her to Massachusetts with their young son, Steve, and the next year was himself invited to offer courses for the school, while he helped re-establish the Evangelical Theological Society's Northeast section, serving two years as its chair and four years as its programmer, and co-planting Pilgrim Church, today a union church of the Conservative Congregational Christian Conference (4Cs) and the Cumberland Presbyterian Church (CPC). He remains its Founding Pastor of Encouragement. He also completed his Doctor of Theology (ThD) degree in Theology and Ancient Literature at Boston University School of Theology. He is the author of more than two hundred articles, stories, poems, chapters in books, reviews, editorials, and with his wife writes the blog *Applying Biblical Truths Today*. He is also author, co-author or co-editor of sixteen books, including two titles in city ministry, *Reaching for the New Jerusalem: A Theological and Biblical Framework for the City* with Gordon-Conwell/Boston professors, and *Name in the Papers* (a novel), which was awarded The Golden Halo Award for Outstanding Contribution to Literature by the Southern California Motion Picture Council. In all, he has won twenty writing and editing awards, and was nominated for an Edgar Award for *Mysterium and Mystery: The Clerical Crime Novel*, an adaptation of his doctoral dissertation from the Mystery Writers of America. That book and *Chanting Down Babylon: The Rastafari Reader* are considered the definitive works in their fields. He is listed in *Contemporary Authors, Who's Who in Religion*, and other such volumes.

DR. VIRGINIA WARD serves as the Assistant Dean of the Boston Campus and Assistant Professor of Youth and Leadership Development at Gordon-Conwell Theological Seminary. She is responsible for facilitating the development of leadership skills and managing urban collaborative field experiences for students. Virginia's local and national involvement in the training and development of youth leaders spans three decades. She teaches youth ministry, leadership and ministry development courses, along with providing spiritual formation support on the Boston Campus.

Dr. Ward comes with extensive experience as an urban pastor, ministry organizer, and youth ministry expert. After an initial study in Management at Northeastern University and courses at Harvard Extension School, Dr. Ward pursued education in ministry, earning her Diploma in Urban Ministries, Master of Arts in Youth Ministry, and Doctor of Ministry in Emerging Generations, all at Gordon-Conwell. A third-generation minster, Rev. Ward is an Associate Pastor at Abundant Life Church where her husband Bishop Lawrence Ward is the Senior Pastor.

Among the many ministry organizations Dr. Ward has served are: DeVos Urban Leadership Initiative (Boston City Coordinator, Coach for Pittsburgh, San Diego, Detroit and New York; Trainer, 1997-present), Black Ministerial Alliance (Trainer and Consultant, 2005-2011), Inter-Varsity (New England's Black Campus Ministries Director and Consultant, 2007-present), and Orange (Keynote Speaker and Workshop Leader, 2014-present).

Virginia resides in Boston with her husband and two adult sons.

GEMMA WENGER received her Bachelor of Arts degree in Economics from the University of California, Los Angeles, her teaching credential from California State College Northridge (CSUN) and her Master of Arts in Educational Administration from National University. She specializes in several areas of educational administration including Special Education, Cross Cultural Language and Academic Development (CLAD), and Intervention, and has served in education in many capacities including Assistant Principal Elementary Instructional Specialist (APEIS), Assistant Principal over Intervention and at Risk students (APRLA), Title I/Bilingual Coordinator, and Literacy Coach. Gemma Wenger was asked to contribute to this dialogue as she possesses strong leadership qualities and is able collaboratively to create a vision as well as a culture and climate whereby all stakeholders are working together to attain a goal. Her success has been centered on her ability to develop and lead professional development for all staff; to identify and implement effective teaching strategies that support the needs of ELLs, SELs, and SPED students, and to analyze data to inform instruction. Gemma has participated in the LAUSD blended learning program, which includes LEXIA, ST Math, Project Based Learning, teaching science through inquiry, investigation, and experimentation, and the district Classroom Technology Project in order to support teachers in their effective implementation of the Common Core Standards.

From ministering in prisons and on skid row, former child actress Gemma Wenger has expanded her ministry to churches, radio, books, newspapers, evangelical outreaches, music, television ministry and currently, she has her own production company. She preached at the Hollywood Bowl Easter Sunrise Service produced by the Trinity Broadcasting Network (TBN) and televised worldwide, and has also made multiple guest appearances on various TBN shows.

Currently, Gemma can be heard every Saturday evening at 11:00 p.m. on KKLA 99.5FM or livestreaming on the internet on kkla.com, and via satellite on The Cross TV Wednesdays at 5:30 p.m. or on thecrosstv. com. After numerous appearances on TBN, Gemma developed her own shows, Gemma Wenger's Hollywood and Beauty for Ashes, currently airing worldwide on Spectrum Cable, The Cross TV, Isaac Television, UP-Lift TV, Jadoo Television, Roku, and YouTube@GemmaWenger. She also has held biweekly church meetings in the Los Angeles area for the past twenty-seven years.

To view Gemma Wenger's program, see thecrosstv.com, LA36.org, YouTube@GemmaWenger, gemmawenger.com, and KKLA.com. To contact Gemma to speak or minister, visit gemmawenger.com.

Bibliography

"Attention Deficit Disorder." https://www.merriam-webster.com/dictionary/attention%20 deficit%20disorder.

Alexander, Robin. "Dialogue Teaching." http://www.robinalexander.org.uk/dialogic-teaching/.

Annas, Aaron Daniel. "Story Telling as Teaching." http://teachinginhighered.com/podcast/storytelling/.

Angelo, Thomas K. and Patricia Cross. *Classroom Assessment Techniques*. 2nd Edition. San Francisco: Jossey-Bass, 1993. http://www.usf.edu/atle/documents/handout-interactive-techniques.pdf.

"Autism." http://learnersdictionary.com/definition/autism.

"Awareness: Evidence for an Advantage of Bilingualism in Dyslexia." http://www.atheme.eu/publications/morphological-awareness-evidence-for-an-advantage-of-bilingualism-in-dyslexia-june-2017/.

Brown, Robert McAfee. *The Essential Reinhold Niebuhr: Selected Essays and Addresses*. New Haven: Yale University Press, 1986.

Buber, Martin. *I and Thou*. New York: Scribner's, 1958.

"CBS Newsflash from Nov. 22nd 1963 Re: The JFK Assassination," https://youtu.be/c7fCpdvcl7k.

Cherry, Kendra. "Erik Erikson's Stages of Psychosocial Development." *https://www.verywell.com/erik-eriksons-stages-of-psychosocial-development-2795740.*

Ciurczak, Peter. "Boston's Foreign Born Population: A Breakdown." https://www.bostonindicators.org/blog/2017/april/the-foreign-born-of-boston.

"Classroom Management Definition." *edglossary.org/classroom-management.*

Clotfelter, Charles T., Helen F. Ladd, and Jacob L. Vigdor. "How and Why Do Teacher Credentials Matter for Student Achievement?" *https://pdfs.semanticscholar.org/448e/2b0e8b8054cc2000ec7f8f0c0b6ccbc76ec2.pdf.*

Daman, Steve. "EGC's Research Uncovers the Quiet Revival." *Inside EGC* 20:4 (November-December 2013).

Daman, Steve. "Understanding Boston's Quiet Revival." *Emmanuel Research Review* 94 (December 2013-January 2014).

DeFazio, Jeanne and John P. Lathrop. *Creative Ways to Build Christian Community*. Eugene: Wipf and Stock, 2013.

Delaney, Maria. "Teacher Stress, Well-being and Stress Management: Taking Care of Yourself So That You Can Take Care of Your Students." https://www.teachingenglish.

org.uk/article/teacher-stress-well-being-stress-management-taking-care-yourself-so-you-can-take-care-yourself.

"Dyslexia," https://www.merriam-webster.com/dictionary/dyslexia.

Eber, Charlene. Review of *The Energy of Forgiveness: Lessons from Those in Restorative Dialogue* by Mark S. Umbreit, Jennifer Blevins, and Ted lewis. *Africanus Journal 9:1 (April 2017)*, 47.

Freire, Paulo. *Pedagogy of the Oppressed*. London: Bloomsbury Academic, 2014.

Fulghum, Robert. *To Know I Learned In Kindergarten*. New York: Ballantine Books, 1986.

Garcia, Maria Ramirez. "Usage of Multi-Media Visual Aids in the English Language Classroom: A Case Study at Margarita Salas Secondary School." https://www.ucm.es/data/cont/docs/119-2015-03-17-11.MariaRamirezGarcia2013.pdf.

Gilbert, Ann Green. "Brain Dance." http://www.creativedance.org/about/braindance/

Gordon-Conwell's Vision, Mission and Purpose. http://www.gordonconwell.edu/about/Mission-and-Purpose.cfm).

Hallowell, Ned. *Crazy Busy*. New York: Ballantine Books, 2006.

Hallowell, Ned. *Driven to Distraction*. New York: Simon and Schuster, 2003.

Hallowell, Ned. *Super Parenting for ADD*. New York: Random House, 2008.

Hannaford, Carla. *Smart Why Learning Is Not All In Your Head*. Salt Lake City: Great River Books, 2007.

Harlow, Caroline Wolf. "Education and Correctional Populations." https://www.bjs.gov/index.cfm?ty=pbdetail&iid=814.

Horowitz, Sheldon H. "Nonverbal Learning Disabilities: A Primer." http://www.ncld.org/types-learning-disabilities/adhd-related-issues/autism-spectrum-disorders/nonverbal-learning-disabilities.

"I Have Dyslexia, What Does It Mean?" http://dyslexia.yale.edu/whatisdyslexia.html.

"Is Cramming for a Test Effective." https://sites.psu.edu/siowfa15/2015/10/09/is-cramming-for-a-test-effective/.

Jensen, Eric. *Teaching with the Brain in Mind*. Kissimmee: Association for Supervision & Curriculum Development, 2005.

Joiner, Reggie. *The Orange Strategy: Reimagine What Your Church Does for Kids and Teenagers*. Cumming: ReThink Group, Inc., 2016.

Kawasaki, Masahiro, Yohei Yamada, Yosuke Ushiku, Eri Miyauchi, and Yoko Yamaguchi. "Scientific Reports, Inter-brain synchronization during coordination of speech rhythm in human-to-human social interaction." https://www.nature.com/articles/srep01692.

Kruschewsky, Gabriel. "Multilingual Benefits That You Only Get If You Speak Another Language." http://www.huffingtonpost.com/2014/06/02/multilingual-benefits_n_5399980.html.

Lieberman, Gerald and Linda Hoody. "Closing the Achievement Gap. Using the Environment as an Integrating Context for Learning. Executive Summary." *http://www.seer.org/extras/execsum.pdf*.

"Making a Great First Impression." https://www.mindtools.com/CommSkll/FirstImpressions.htm.

Manto, M. and P. Jissendi. "Cerebellum: links between development, developmental disorders and motor learning." https://www.ncbi.nlm.nih.gov/pmc/articles/PMC3263706/.

Maslow, Abraham *(1943)*. "A Theory of Human Motivation," *originally published in Psychological Review 50 (4): 370–96. doi: 10.1037/h0054346, posted on line by*

Christopher D. Green, "Classics in the History of Psychology." York University, Toronto, Ontario, http://psychclassics.yorku.ca/Maslow/motivation.htm

McGlynn, Angela. "Successful Beginnings for College Teaching." http://www.usf.edu/atle/documents/handout-interactive-techniques.pdf.

Miller, Greg. "Music Builds Bridges in the Brain." http://www.sciencemag.org/news/2008/04/music-builds-bridges-brain.

Morrison-Shetlar and Alison/Mary Marwitz. "Teaching Creatively: Ideas in Action." http://www.usf.edu/atle/documents/handout-interactive-techniques.pdf.

"Offering Structure and Support in the Language Classroom." https://sites.educ.ualberta.ca/staff/olenka.bilash/Best%20of%20Bilash/structuresupport.html.

Radcliffe, R. and G. McKoon. "Modeling the Effects of Repetition and Word Frequency." https://www.researchgate.net/publication/229233853_Bias_Effects_in_Perceptual_Identification_A_Neuropsychological_Investigation_of_the_Role_of_Explicit_Memory.

Ratey, John. Spark. Boston: Little, Brown and Company, 2013.

Shenandoah, April. Review of Just Peace: Ecumenical, Intercultural and Interdisciplinary Perspectives edited by Fernando Enns and Annette Mosher. Africanus Journal 9:2 (November 2017), 59.

Siegfredsen, Jane Williams. "Danish Forest Schools." http://www.teachearlyyears.com/enabling-environments/view/danish-forest-schools.

"Socratic Teaching." https://www.criticalthinking.org/pages/socratic-teaching/606.

Silberman, Mel. "Active Learning: 101 Strategies to Teach Any Subject." http://www.usf.edu/atle/documents/handout-interactive-techniques.pdf.

St. Clair, Robert N. and Howard Giles. The Social and Psychological Context of Language. Hillsdale: Lawrence Erlebaum Associates, 1982.

Strohman, Johannah. "Methods for Teaching Hispanic English Language Learners." http://digitalcommons.liberty.edu/cgi/viewcontent.cgi?article=1335&context=honors.

Sulaiman, Hasan and Jussein Qashoa. "English Writing Anxiety: Alleviating Strategies." www.sciencedirect.com/science/article/pii/S1877042814037690.

"Teachers as Role Models." https://teach.com/what/teachers-change-lives/teachers-are-role-models/.

"Teaching and Learning Programme." http://learning.gov.wales/docs/learningwales/publications/140801-multi-sensory-learning-en.pdf.

"The Importance of Effective Communication." http://singteach.nie.edu.sg/issue50-people/.

The Pew Research Center. "13.4% of the population of the United States was born in a foreign country." http://www.pewhispanic.org/2017/05/03/facts-on-u-s-immigrants-current-data/.

Tomatis, Alfred. The Voice and the Ear. Lanham: Rowman & Littlefield, 2004.

Van Gundy, Arthur. 101 Activities for Teaching Creativity and Problem Solving. Pfeiffer: San Francisco, 2005. http://www.usf.edu/atle/documents/handout-interactive-techniques.pdf.

Villafañe, Eldin. Seek the Peace of the City: Reflections on Urban Ministry. Wm. B. Eerdmans, 1995.

Walters, Shipley. From Pantry to Food Bank: The First Forty Years: A History of the Food Bank. Bloomington: Author House, 2010.

Watkins, Ryan. *75 e-Learning Activities: Making Online Learning Interactive.* San Francisco: Pfeiffer, 2005. http://www.usf.edu/atle/documents/handout-interactive-techniques.pdf.

"Who are Urban Students? Pedagogy in Action." http://serc.carleton.edu/sp/library/urban/who.html.

"What if Learning? A Christian Way of Teaching." http://www.whatiflearning.com/the-approach/strategies-for-seeing-anew/full-document.

Wills, Howard P., Wendy M. Iwaszuk, Debra Kamps, and Emily Shumate. *Education & Treatment of Children.* 37.2 (May 2014): 191.

Wu, Dr. Ge. "Biomechanical Analysis of Tai Chi Quan Movement." http://www.uvm.edu/cnhs/rms/profiles/ge_wu_phd.

Yolo County Food Bank. http://www.yolofoodbank.org/.

Subject Index

Adult Basic Education (ABE), 55
Africanus Guild, 113
Africanus Journal, 106
Africanus Monograph Series, 114
Agosto, Efrain, 110
Alexander, Robin, 98
Athanasian Scholar, 75–76, 91–92, 112–14, 116–17, 124
Athanasius, 112, 114

Bel Air School, 19, 32
Bettenhausen, Elizabeth, 109
Blooms Taxonomy, 31
Boston Public Library, 55
Boston University School of Theology, 109
Brooks, Katherine, 37

Cal State Teach English Language Learners Program, 81
Center for Urban Ministerial Education at Gordon-Conwell Theological Seminary Boston Campus (CUME), 110, 138
Chávez, César, 82
Classroom Management, 21, 35, 37
Cognitive Coaching, 23
Cronkite, Walter, 78
Cross-Cultural Language and Academic Development (CLAD), 33

Darling, Sharon, 109, 128
Davis Joint Unified School District, 81
DeFazio, Inez, 81
DeFazio, Michelle, 79

Depth of Knowledge Levels, 31
Dialogical Teaching, 93
Dual Language Two-Way Immersion, 28

Eber, Charlene, 87
English as a Foreign Language (TOEFL), 55
English Language Arts, 18–19, 21, 23, 25, 27, 30
English Language Development (ELD), 29
English Language Learner, 18, 20, 23, 30, 42, 44, 51, 54, 67, 75, 76, 92, 105, 107, 110, 139
English Only (EO), 29
ESL program, 54–55, 58
Evangelical Theological Society (ETS), 114

Fort Apache, 36

General Educational Development (GED), 56, 110–11
Gonzalez, Fernando, 59
Gordon-Conwell Theological Seminary (GCTS), 75

Hall, Doug, 140
Hamilton-Wenham Public Library, 57
Haverhill Public Library, 56
Holistic Teaching, 95
Immigration and Naturalization Act of 1965, 139
Independent Work Time (IWT), 26
Initially Fluent English Proficient Students (IFEPS), 29

Scripture Index